The Wonderful World of Widowhood...

Except When It Isn't

JUDY TOWNE JENNINGS M.A. ED., PT

WESTBOW
PRESS®
A DIVISION OF THOMAS NELSON
& ZONDERVAN

Scripture quotations marked (NIV) are taken from the Holy Bible, New International Version®, NIV®. Copyright © 1973, 1978, 1984, 2011 by Biblica, Inc.™ Used by permission of Zondervan. All rights reserved worldwide. www.zondervan.com The "NIV" and "New International Version" are trademarks registered in the United States Patent and Trademark Office by Biblica, Inc.

Scripture quotations are from the ESV® Bible (The Holy Bible, English Standard Version®), copyright © 2001 by Crossway, a publishing ministry of Good News Publishers. Used by permission. All rights reserved.

WestBow Press books may be ordered through booksellers or by contacting:

WestBow Press
A Division of Thomas Nelson & Zondervan
1663 Liberty Drive
Bloomington, IN 47403
www.westbowpress.com
844-714-3454

Because of the dynamic nature of the Internet, any web addresses or links contained in this book may have changed since publication and may no longer be valid. The views expressed in this work are solely those of the author and do not necessarily reflect the views of the publisher, and the publisher hereby disclaims any responsibility for them.

Any people depicted in stock imagery provided by Getty Images are models, and such images are being used for illustrative purposes only.
Certain stock imagery © Getty Images.

ISBN: 978-1-9736-2101-0 (sc)
ISBN: 978-1-9736-2100-3 (e)

Print information available on the last page.

WestBow Press rev. date: 09/09/2020

DEDICATIONS

To God, my Father, who knows what I need before I know I need it.

To Another, whose unconditional love healed my Soul

ACKNOWLEDGEMENT

Thank you to all my widow friends.
Their determination to recreate themselves after they
emerge from the Tunnel of Grief is energizing.

Contents

DOOR FOUR
Becoming Butterflies

DOOR FIVE
Learning to Love Oneself

DOOR SIX
Adventures With God

Introduction

This book is a revision of the book that I wrote and published in 2018. The primary reason for revising it is to authenticate the events and the miracles. It was originally presented in the third person with a heroine rather than as my personal story. Unfortunately, some of the miracles presented were dismissed as literary hyperbole. I understand that audibly hearing God speak to me may be difficult to accept as real! But it happened as did all the other miracles I have related.

This is not the typical grief book with a scholarly format. Although I am a physical therapist, this information is much more informal. I write as if I am sitting across the table from a new friend having a cup of coffee. I have shared my grief experiences and how I dealt with the forced changes in my life via a series of mini-stories serving as strategic rocks placed across a stream. Hopefully my stories will offer a path forward for others.

One of the primary themes in this book is that God is real and does work directly in the lives of his 'children'. In all sincerity, this book has no value if my friend, God, is not real. I do not apologize for claiming that God interacts in my personal life on a regular basis. The storyline is built around real experiences and unexplainable 'miracles' (God-moments) that moved me from a broken woman to a woman who happens to be widowed...from a complacent Christian to someone claiming a powerful relationship with God, Christ, and the Holy Spirit. If I can have this cherished friendship, anyone can! My intent is to offer other widowed seniors a chance for adventures orchestrated by God. If they are able to accept their losses and make the adjustments necessary…if they can learn to love themselves again and step out with faith, they may find that life can be better, maybe even Wonderful

I compared the journey of a widow emerging from the Tunnel of Grief to the metamorphosis of a butterfly out of the cocoon. Not every widow gets sufficient help from friends, churches, or counselors to be able to make the adjustments needed to be whole again. Making the necessary choices requires individual effort and can be difficult just as it takes work for the butterfly. I have chosen to share both the bad and the good to let my readers know that I understand, "I have been there!" For some that will offer the needed permission to make changes.

The last theme is the boldest. I believe that God is all about love from the core of one's being. We as a society should be willing to encourage widows and widowers to find a dynamic source of unconditional love, possibly another spouse. So often widows are advised never to date, nor to hope to be kissed passionately again. The need for passionate love does not have an expiration date. I have described how our widows support group provided mentoring to help those with an interest date safely.

I am interested in reactions. This book will work well in a discussion format which is how I gleaned much of the information. There are discussion questions offered at the end to help a group grow together.

My intent is to offer other widowed seniors a chance for adventures orchestrated by God. If they are able to accept their losses and make the adjustments necessary…if they can learn to love themselves again and step out with faith, they may find that life can be better, maybe even Wonderful.

God Bless,

Judy Towne Jennings
Judytownejennings@gmail.com

DOOR ONE

When One Door Closes, Another Door Opens

It takes courage to close some of our life-
doors: chapters, stages, phases, periods.
It takes more courage to step through the next
door to see what might be waiting.

Chapter 1

Endings Are New Beginnings

2010
January

Life as a caregiver has reached a stable routine for me. Dean had a terrible 2009. He experienced hospitalizations, periods of suffering pain, and days of frightening hallucinations that aliens were attacking. This January, that seems to be behind him. Although weak, his days are comfortable if not pleasant. This journaled letter reflects this time of reprieve for both of us.

Dear God,

One of my new pieces of wisdom: life's events are always relative. At this stage of our lives as a couple, Dean and I are living a series of mundane daily routines. He remains awake for very short amounts of time before he needs another nap. When awake, he needs my undivided attention. Those needs have become the time markers of my day.

Other than Dean, I have no great commitments anymore. I am content at this stage in our marriage. Despite his continuous decline, both physically and mentally, there are moments of great satisfaction spliced into the mediocre. Occasionally he comes up with a witty response or a very tender comment. On a good day, we share a deep conversation. Yesterday, we talked about questions he would ask his father when he sees him on the other side.

I wish I had his acceptance of this debilitating disease. When I ask him if he is sad, he responds that we just need to make the best of each day. And most of the time he is placid in spite of his continual decline.

I pray that You will continue to hold us both as we persevere in this fight against Lewy Body Dementia. Without You, Lord, we are an out of control snowball rolling downhill.

Your little child

As I had experienced on so many other evenings after pouring my heart out to the divine presence inspiring me to stay strong, I was encouraged by these responsive thoughts that I typed into the computer. I have never understood how these thoughts surfaced in my mind after I reached out to my God, but I am thankful that they did. Unfailingly all my responsive entries have provided me with a sense of peace and a feeling of being loved.

Dear Little Child,

You are seeing the roses along the path. You are gaining a pearl of wisdom that will serve you well in the months to come. Life will not always be as peaceful as your days are right now, but be assured that I will be there with you. I wish Dean did not have to walk this walk, but in My wisdom, I know that this is the road he must take.

Continue to talk to him about Me, and about Jesus, and about the good that he has done in his life. He is a success and has lived his life to his credit. He needs to learn to trust Me more and to have more confidence in his God-given abilities. But that is for another time.

I have prepared you for this journey with the passing of Dean's parents and then yours. You have all the tools you need to forge ahead. I do not have any work for you to do right now, except to do your best each day to care for Dean and for your own needs.

Keep your heart open. Keep your words to Dean positive and edifying. Your words can be as piercing as a sharp sword, and the wounds do not heal quickly. That is My only admonition for tonight. People are watching you. Be a good teacher.

Love, your Friend

2010
May

A flood is a powerful way of stating that I had no control over the events in Dean's life. We got caught in the flood of May 1, 2010, in Nashville. The unfolding of the events was surreal as if unseen forces directed our comings and goings.

We had driven to the Nashville area to visit with AJ and Caryn and see our granddaughter and new grandson. Since Dean had needed less help the prior month, I agreed to the five-hour trip. To be sure we could accommodate Dean's physical limitations on stairs, I made a reservation for us to stay in a timeshare condo north of town rather than sleep in an upstairs bedroom at AJ's. I was very pleased with myself for making plans that would support all of Dean's needs while giving us the opportunity to visit easily with the kids.

On the afternoon of April 30th, the whole family was enjoying a great cookout on AJ's patio when a chain of tornadoes and a wall of rain began to come through. Four adults, two babies, and three dogs squeezed into a tiny closet under the stairs gave me a severe sense of dread. Once the path was clear on the radar report, I packed Dean into our car and headed north, back to our hotel and his medications. What should have been an easy 25-minute ride up Route 24 turned into an hour-long dangerous trek. Like two pioneers crossing the wilderness, I was required to take a circuitous route to find open roads. Flooding was obvious everywhere. We made it, and Dean settled in comfortably for the night. The weather channel assured all of Nashville that the worst was over. I expected to sleep late before heading back to AJ's house Sunday afternoon.

What the reporters didn't say was that the flood commission had to open river channels further north to prevent extensive water damage. It was a calculated risk that Nashville would be able to handle the extra water. As I stood with the other onlookers on the second-floor landing watching the waters quickly rise around all the cars in the parking lot, I felt completely baffled. There was no warning for the second rise in the waters, nor did we have any time to pack a quick bag and get to our car.

For the next 24 hours, an anxious group of hotel guests banded together waiting to be evacuated. This was almost too much for me to handle. Seeing the muddy floodwater pour into my new car just beneath my balcony was trivial compared with my concern for my frail husband. What would this traumatic experience do to him? On some days during the previous month, he had become anxious when breakfast was five minutes late, and he continued to have nightmares about aliens and monsters at least once a week. His Lewy Body Dementia looked like Parkinson's Disease physically but could act like Alzheimer's cognitively. Symptoms of LBD fluctuated. Dean could wake in the morning with crystal clear reasoning and normal motor skills. The next day he might attempt to eat a plastic bread tie if I had my back turned. Waiting for an evacuation from a flood was a bit more challenging than making sure he had healthy snacks at the table to keep him busy until his plate of food arrived.

Monday afternoon, boats began coming in to rescue those stranded. Ours was a flat-hulled fishing boat. Perfect strangers helped load our belongings, while others literally lifted Dean and his wheelchair into the boat from the second story landing. As we began the ride to dry land, I whispered to Dean what an eerie feeling it was to be floating over the tops of submerged cars and semi-trucks.

Our frazzled son met us at the evacuation site and took us back to his home. We had to stay there for ten days while the insurance claim on the car was processed, and I could gather the rest of our belongings from a warehouse off site. Neither of us could relax nor fathom what we had just experienced.

2010
July

My anxiety and Dean's nightmares escalated after the flood disaster.

Dear God,

I have needed You more this month than usual, and You have always been there. I don't question the overall thread of my life, but I sure have confusions regarding the day-to-day.

I am beginning to understand that You had a purpose for us going through the flood experience, and I accept the loss of the car. Too many serendipitous events occurred to assure me that we needed to be where we were when the waters rose. One of those events was allowing the couple on the first floor, Carolyn and Fred, to move to high ground in our one-bedroom condo on the second floor. I thought we were being good neighbors, helping strangers find safety in the storm. In reality, they were invaluable the next day when I needed to evacuate Dean and all his medical tote bags into the rescue boat. They held me together when I just wanted to stand on the balcony and scream.

Please don't misunderstand what I am trying to say. I do appreciate Your caring presence as I manage Dean's decline.

The truth is that my strength is failing, Lord; I don't know how much longer I can do this. He is gravely different since we came back home: more confused, more fatigued, and less capable with any task. Many mornings he needs all my strength to get him into the wheelchair.

You have assured me that You know I am doing the best that I can.

Unfortunately, it is so much more difficult than I ever imagined caring for another person would ever be.

I need help, Lord, and I need it soon; or there won't be much left of me to take care of either of us.

Your Dear One

I am here. And I am always here, and I joyously accept your confusion and questions. First in the order of your letter: the flood. It was necessary to move Dean to a more advanced level. I have told you before that his work on earth is almost done. There is a process to get him from being with you to transitioning to Heaven. From earthly perspectives, that means more deterioration of the body and mind until he is ready to leave. He is not there yet. So often this is looked at as a bad thing. "Your husband has taken a turn for the worse." From a Heavenly perspective, passing over is like a snake shedding its skin. Dean will leave the old useless, worn out body covering behind and stretch into a new shiny appearance...more useful, efficient, and sturdy than he has ever had before. Be assured that this passage to be with Me is real, and I am real.

Next, I will defuse your frustration about the particulars of the flood and loss of the car. As much as you try, you can't know what will happen in the future. You truly felt it was in Dean's best interest to go back to the hotel.

You can call the serendipitous intercessions Godly assistance if you want. Some people would call them coincidences. The important thing is that you had the help you needed when you needed it. Since going through the flood

wasn't optional, I sent you some cushions in the form of helpful people to fall back on. And I know you accepted the situation even if you joked about being angry with Me for several days afterward.

Now about your primary question: Dean's decreased function and the future. You will not be told the particulars of his next steps. Again, you will need to trust. But I can assure you that I don't expect you to go through the stages alone. I will provide just who and what you need in every phase of his journey. As to your question of whether or not you have the strength to persevere throughout this journey; I honor your strength whatever it may be, and 'pray' that you find the reserves to do what needs to be done with continuing compassion.

That should cover it. You are doing fine.

Love, your friend

2010
September

Dear God,

It is 2 AM with another night of rambling thoughts. During the day, I can be upbeat and confident. I suppose I appear to have everything under control; when literally, my life structures are falling down around me. Dean has had a terrible summer. Each month, he became more vulnerable, less able to walk, and more confused. Medicare no longer covered the nursing visits every week. When I asked for a hospice evaluation, the doctor turned us down. I am wallowing in this misery by myself, and I greatly fear I am missing something that would help Dean's quality of life. Thank goodness, the occupational therapist, an expert in Parkinson Plus diseases, is coming tomorrow. Maybe she has some answers for us.

Dear God

Thank You for sending Miss Deidra into our lives. She was wonderful with Dean today. When he told her that his goal was to get back to playing tennis, she was gently supportive. He felt validated as a person!

When she and I were alone, she told me that she was astounded at how well he communicated and attempted to do everything she had asked. Her first reaction was to classify him as only moderately affected in all his skills, but as we talked, she adjusted her opinion. "Judy, you have obviously done a superb job with him. He appears in much better health than he truly is. I have to be honest and tell you that he is near the final stages of the disease. Without you, he would be bedfast in a nursing home. There is no other therapy to make him better than what you are doing. Keep on with whatever you have been doing."

It was strangely comforting, God, for someone to be honest with me and validate what I was suspecting. Miss Deidra was exceptionally well versed in diseases that look like Parkinson's but are something else. She answered all my questions without stealing my hope. It seems so strange to be thanking You for sending me a person who had to give me such a negative report, but she did so with such compassion. In reality, knowing where we are in this process was very helpful. If I really can't carry on, I know I can call her, and she will find help.

Chapter 2

"No Problem"

2010
October

God provided a multitude of mini-miracles throughout the intense last three years of Dean's life. Lest there be any doubt that I was being held together by the hands of a Supreme Being, He orchestrated a mighty miracle during the last few days of Dean's life.

Two weeks after the occupational therapy evaluation, I heard a loud thump coming from Dean's room early one Friday morning. Somehow, I knew this was serious, maybe the beginning of the end. Dean was sprawled on the floor beside the bed. How he got over the protective railing attached to the bed, I would never know.

For three years, I had been able to handle all his symptoms from the perspective of an efficient physical therapist. Whenever he had another problem, I would effectively 'fix' it. Not this time. Seeing him lying in an awkward position on the floor with fear written all over his face, forced me to react like any other wife. I panicked!

Although he was in no pain and fully alert, something was drastically different. When I tried to help him sit and get to his knees, just as we had done many times before, he had no strength in his legs. They were like two noodles as soon as he tried to bear any weight.

A rational person would have called the EMT's for help. Being utterly irrational at that moment, I somehow muscled a 200-pound man back into bed. My mind kept saying, "He shouldn't be on the floor! He shouldn't be this weak! If I can just get him back into bed, everything will be okay. He will be normal! This will all go away!"

Once in bed, he did relax and fall asleep. Not so for me. As I sat at the kitchen table sipping a cup of coffee, trying to calm my nerves, I realized I needed answers and made the decision to call the emergency squad.

When the results of X-Rays and lab work came back, the doctor pulled me aside to tell me that he had checked every orifice and system for the possible cause of Dean's overwhelming decline in function, and he could find nothing. He was sorry to tell me that he felt it was an advancement of the disease. The doctor admitted Dean so that I could get arrangements made for more help at home.

Dean seemed to respond to the fluids and rest on Saturday and was able to converse with family. Unfortunately, on Sunday he was bed-fast, glassy-eyed, and unable to recognize anyone who came to visit. When I returned at 6:00 AM on Monday, I could not wake him. Our doctor agreed that Dean was in a coma, and needed a hospice unit. He was transferred later that day.

Dean and I had prepared for this inescapable event. Earlier in the summer, we had discussed final arrangements. Both of us felt that donating his brain (and body) to the research division of the University of Cincinnati was a good idea. Maybe exploring the monster at work in his body would help develop a treatment for the next person.

Unfortunately, I procrastinated with his signing of the papers requesting the donation. When I presented all of my Power of Attorney papers to the Hospice Unit head nurse on Tuesday morning, the nurse informed me that body donation could only occur when the donor had given his written permission to do so. Therefore, my power of attorney was null and void in this situation. After exploring options with the social worker and the Head of the University donation program, I was devastated. I realized that I had a significant problem. Without his signed permission, his body would be sent to a funeral home and put into a holding vault for upwards of 6 months. It could take the donor program committee that long to determine whether to accept him or not.

The alternative was to use a local funeral home and forget the donation plan. Either option felt like a kick in the gut. This was a dilemma that I had not anticipated. Even though I had been methodical with every phase of Dean's care for five years, the procrastination with the final arrangements made me feel utterly worthless as Dean's caregiver. There was apparently nothing I could do to "fix" this problem.

In the past, it seemed that God had done His best work when all hope was lost. As I sat in the alcove next to Dean's room wondering what I was going to do, our pastor walked around the corner and said, "Guess who I am talking to in the next room?" I was surprised to see him because I had not seen him arrive.

"Who?" I asked.

"Dean," he exclaimed.

"No Way!"

"Yup, he is wide awake."

"What a miracle! Let's get those papers signed," I exclaimed, as I rushed toward the room.

When I walked into Dean's room, he was resting comfortably with his head elevated on the pillow. Although his eyes were closed, his breathing was normal. Amazingly, he looked relatively healthy for someone in a hospice bed. As I leaned toward him, he turned to look at me and smiled.

I put my hand lovingly on his arm, "Sweetie, you are awake! Can you sign these papers for the donation program at the University?" I asked as I laid the papers on the bedside table across his chest.

"Sure!" he responded as if he had been patiently waiting for me to ask.

Breathing a huge sigh of relief, I left to find the social worker and nurse while the Pastor continued to visit with Dean. He was still alert when the three of us entered his room. When I placed the pen in his fingers, he could barely hold on to it, and he apparently was not able to see well.

"Where do you want me to sign?" I moved his hand with the pen to the line.

"Am I on the right spot?" He asked.

"Yes, go ahead and sign."

As he put the pen down on the table, the social worker asked, "Do you know who you are?"

"Certainly, I am Dean Allen Jennings," he responded emphatically.

"That is good enough for me," she commented and signed the form as a required witness.

Fully aware that Dean had not had food or drink in three days, the head nurse inquired of his needs, "Mr. Jennings, are you hungry?"

"Nope. I am just fine," he answered enthusiastically.

"Are you thirsty?"

"Nope. I am just fine."

With that, he closed his eyes and gently slid back into the depths of the coma. Dean lasted five more days but never again regained consciousness.

Having thought about this sequence of events in-depth, I feel certain that Dean's spirit knew I was in deep trouble.

God, I think You said to him, "Sorry, Son, your work is not quite done. You have one more, big task to do. Your wife is in trouble. You need to sign the release form." And Dean responded, "No problem!"

DOOR TWO

Experiencing the Not-So-Wonderful World of Widowhood

The Magic of the 'Coats' of Widowhood is that they can provide
a suitable outer appearance while effectively concealing
a widow's internal brokenness.

Chapter 3

My First 'Coat' Of Widowhood

2012

From My Journal Notes Regarding My First Two Years of Widowhood

> "Looking back, I acknowledge that one definition of a widow is a woman whose husband has died. I became a widow the second that Dean ceased breathing in the hospice room; but, I certainly didn't grasp the impact of that moment for weeks and months. There is a difference between a status on paper and the acceptance of that status in daily living. I couldn't even voice the word 'widow' for two months."

For the first five weeks after Dean passed, I stayed with my son, AJ, and his family, five hours away from my home. The day after Dean's Memorial, we all traveled from Fairfield to their new house as part of a job change. Helping to care for the two small children kept my mind busy. My granddaughter was almost two and my grandson was nine months. As the two adults unpacked and settled into jobs, I played with and loved-on babies!

The moment that I actually realized I needed a widowhood 'Coat' was when I returned home to face a two-month mountain of bills. Most were the usual, but the phone bill was exorbitant: $458 instead of my usual $60. It sucked the air right out of my lungs when I saw the amount.

I put on a 'Coat' to do battle during the 15-minute hold while I waited to talk to the customer service representative for the phone company.

"What can I do for you, Mrs. Jennings?" the lady who took my call asked.

"I don't understand my phone bill this month. These charges are very high."

"Let's see; you owed $200 going into the month and have well over your quota of roaming calls during this period."

"How could I have been $200 in arrears; I pay each month what I was told to pay last February when I opened this account. It is automatically paid by my bank the first of the month."

"Yes, I see that, but your rates have gone up each month since February, and that has continued to accumulate as an unpaid balance."

"Why was this not brought to my attention? I talked to a phone representative in July about something else, and she was reviewing my account. She said nothing about any unpaid balances each month. And what do you mean 'roaming' charges?" I responded with agitation in my voice.

"Whenever you are out of your local area, the calls you make are routed through a different carrier and that generates a charge for that service. You had exceeded your quota of allowed minutes with your plan before you were charged for additional minutes," the phone lady explained.

In total exasperation, I exclaimed, "I am a new widow; my husband passed in October, and I had to make many phone calls while I was staying at my son's!"

"I am so very sorry, Mrs. Jennings. Let me see what we can do!" There was a long pause.

"I have removed all the roaming charges. Your current bill will just be the $200 in normal usage. And again, please accept my condolences. I hope this brightens your day," softly stated the phone representative.

I was astounded at the change in the lady's demeanor. For the first time in two months, I realized there could be a positive side of widowhood. That first 'Coat' was almost a full coat of armor, hefty and uncomfortable. I didn't want it and only put it on to fight the giant phone corporation.

When Ms. Phone Lady had been so kind, I was able to throw off my armor to acknowledge what I had been fighting so hard to deny: I had become a widow.

There is no magic rule for grieving. How a woman reacts to being left behind is entirely personal. One of my widowed friends cried nonstop for two weeks and never left the house. In an effort to stop the pain, her daughter offered horrible advice to hasten an end to her mother's heartbreak. Mabel had cared for her husband for seven years and was having an extremely difficult time letting go. Her 30-year-old daughter, Sally, informed Mabel authoritatively that she should allow herself to grieve no longer than one month. She should then get on with the rest of her life.

This daughter, trying to quell deep pain, caused more harm than help. When Mabel's grief was undaunted after the first month, she felt guilty for her tears and began to pull away from friends and family. The lousy advice made her situation worse. Several of us seasoned widows explained that each heart must heal in its own way and own time.

Two of my other widowed friends began seeing professional counselors to sort out their feelings. One of these widows was also experiencing severe numbness in her chest, neck, and mouth. Fortunately, when she mentioned this to the counselor, she was told that it might help if she took deep breaths frequently throughout the day. In truth, her grief was such that she was literally breathing insufficiently. Within a few days, her breathing had normalized allowing her numbness to dissipate.

I purged our home within days of Dean's passing. This, I realized later, is not an uncommon reaction. For his last three very sick years, I slept in the bedroom across the hall from the master bedroom. After his passing, I became nauseated whenever I entered his bedroom, which prevented me from moving back into the master. Unfortunately, I couldn't sleep well in the second bedroom either. Revitalization of the master bedroom and bath was urgently needed!

I disposed of the mattress and all the old bed linens in the trash and tore out the carpet. After having the room and bathroom painted a soothing color, I could again sleep restfully in the master bedroom. The final touch was placing a stuffed animal pillow against my back to simulate Dean's comforting warmth.

Some women immerse themselves in work.

Some bury their own identity when they bury their spouses.

All reactions during those initial days, weeks, months are efforts to wrap the self in an invisible shroud of sadness: the first 'Coat' of Widowhood.

Hence, to guard the heart, women often feel forced to don figurative protective coverings: 'Coats' to cover the person they have been forced to become. For instance, the Me appearing in public was far different than the Me, crying in bed at night with overwhelming angst. My anger, frustration, even bitterness was not who I once was. Conversely, people might see me as composed, and mentally sharp; when in reality, I could barely last 15 minutes of a 2-hour line dancing class before body and mind would shut down forcing me to leave the session.

In my prayer meditation, I compared my husband's passage out of this life to a snake shedding his worn-out skin (outer covering) as he moved into his next life adventure. This analogy was entirely appropriate for my own metamorphosis as a widow my first year. I needed to shed several types of 'Coats' in my effort to find a new identity. In the next few chapters, I will try to describe a few of the 'Coats' that I needed to wear. I will also explain some of the societal limitations that many widows of today need to deal with and eventually shed.

Chapter 4

The Pity Party 'Coat'

God, this is me. I am having a pity-party, and I need You to listen. Who else can I tell this to?

I am not adjusting well at all to this widow label. As a couple, we shared chores and house tasks. Now I have to do it all! I should have become accustomed after doing everything while Dean was sick. Somehow it is more burdensome now…maybe because I realize that now it is forever.

I don't want to fix toilets, buy a car by myself, or travel alone cross-country to visit family. This wasn't supposed to happen to us. We were supposed to travel and grow old together. As much as I miss him, I would never wish for him to go through that exit again. He did it well and is at peace. It is all the rest that is troubling me.

During my moments of feeling sorry for myself while being a caregiver, I always expected it to be less stressful once I was on my own. No one warned me that life as a widow would require different adjustments. During my daydreams, I would revert back to the Me I was as a single working woman, 40 years ago. "My time would be my own without the need for a job. I could buy any type of groceries I wanted and cook as little as possible. My friends would have similar interests and plenty of time to do fun activities with me.

Those daydreams were extremely naïve! This Aloneness was definitely not on my bucket list. I am tired of being a widow and I want to go back to the life I had with Dean! And I want it Right Now!

As during my caregiving trials, dumping unfiltered raw emotions into the computer seemed to bring forth a semblance of acceptance and comfort, if I would just let the thoughts in my mind surface.

> **My Dear Child,**
>   **As I have mentioned before, you need patience. Be gentle with yourself. All things will work together for the greater good. I will be here to listen to your whining if you need to compile a list of your frustrations. You know you work through things better on paper. Take your time. I am not going anywhere.**
>   **Love, Ever Your Friend**

As usual, my wonderful computer counselor was right. Making an inventory of necessary adjustments helped me identify the areas of my life that I could do something about; as well as, the areas that I would just need to tolerate.

Most of my anger centered on the loss of 'Me' in my life. For five years, Dean's declining health had taken precedence. Once able to focus on my wants and needs, I expected the Old Me to resurface, but that didn't happen. I needed to start over. It was irrelevant whether I liked the Old Me, liked my married persona, or was ready to make massive changes. Reality surrounding my life as a widow, was forcing me to either adjust or sit in the corner and cry all day.

Old Me loved her independence and had no difficulty making big decisions. New Me realized that she hated living alone. Deciding what to eat for breakfast was more than she could handle. It was mentally awful when 'New me' was forced to focus on big tasks. New Me hated refinancing the house by herself, or finding an attorney to fight for her husband's social security benefits.

The change in the way people interacted with me, 'the widow', was the hardest to accept. Who was this person that people were rejecting, manipulating, criticizing, or pitying? It was very difficult to recognize the person they obviously saw. Henry was a prime example. Dean's sweet gentle friend, Henry, was so uncomfortable being alone with a widow, that he wouldn't let 'New me' join him to walk around the block in broad daylight. The same man that had spent hours with Dean the last two years of his life made 'New Me' feel like a brazen hussy for wanting to talk to someone when walking. When he said that he wasn't sure what people would say if they saw him walking with a woman, 'New Me' felt like he had hit her with a shovel. There had been no advance warning on that one.

Even some friends at church became strange. Although I needed hugs to feel like I still mattered, I quickly learned to stay far away from the married men that I had routinely hugged at church when Dean was by my side. That way I didn't get the overly solicitous hugs or evil-eyed stares from their possessive wives. Several wives seemed to question my intentions toward their old out-of-shape husbands.

One night, as I lay in my dark bedroom, I fantasized that someday I would arrive in Tomorrow-Land. A door would open to a room filled with people who genuinely wanted to be friends with the latest and greatest version of me as a person. I fell asleep with a smattering of hope.

Occasionally, there had been breakthroughs that first year. A little self-confidence had resurfaced because I did not succumb to one exuberant outburst from my son. When AJ awakened me with a 6:00 a.m. phone call to share what he thought was a brilliant idea, I was able to listen patiently.

"Mom, I have the perfect solution. You should immediately sell the house and give us the proceeds. We will sell our house and build a bigger house that we can all live in together. That way, you won't be alone, and we can eliminate daycare expenses."

It was a compliment that he wanted me to live with them and be an active grandparent. And his suggestion would be a perfect solution for some widows. I had the wisdom to realize on that call that I desperately wanted my own life and my own space even if I couldn't quite picture what that life looked like.

"Thanks for the offer, but I have been advised not to make any big decisions for at least a year."

Dear God,

I think I am over my pity party. Thanks for always being in the background of my daily dramas. I realize that I had the people I needed to get through the disease, hospice, and the Memorial Service. I am beginning to realize that if I can get through that journey, I can get through anything!

Hmmm, maybe I am beginning to recognize some of my old self in the mirror after all. It might be time to put the pity party 'Coat' in the closet.

Love, Me

Are you done? Good ranting. I am here if you need more time in the ranting box.
Love, Your Constant Friend

Chapter 5

'Coats' Can Help

The value of a coat is determined by a person's need. When the need is met, the person removes the coat. Coats come in all sizes, shapes, styles, colors, fabrics, and purpose. An author could write a whole book about the history and wisdom of coat use.

I recalled that twice on vacations I had had to buy real coats. I failed to take a jacket for the bike ride in upper New York when I vacationed my first summer with Andrea and Barry. The only windbreaker in that small town was bright red, one size too small, and expensive. It was definitely symbolic of how I felt on that first vacation as a widow - angry, conspicuous, uncomfortable, and worried about money. How apropos.

The red coat was the exact opposite of a fleece coat that I bought on a trip with Dean while he was still able to travel. The fleece was one size too big, pink, and only cost $10. It was a symbol of comfort. I had to smile when I realized that wearing the fleece jacket felt like wearing a blanket HUG.

As I dealt with my own reactions to being a widow, I found it interesting to note how other people were reacting to their widowhood. Those widows or widowers who began every sentence with, "When my husband/wife was alive, we would...," seemed to be wearing heavy parkas in the middle of the summer. My two male neighbors were perfect examples. Two years after their wives had passed, they would still launch into bitter recriminations of how the doctors had killed their wives. Their hostility remained just below the surface, seething out with any crack in the conversation. They lived across the street from each other and frequently conversed about their mutual misery.

Because my house was at the end of our cul-de-sac, I needed to pass them frequently. Instead of joining in their "Woe is me!" sidewalk conversations, I put on my friendly, "Can you help me?" 'Coat'. It seemed that if they turned their attention to my needs, they were less negative when all three of us talked. One afternoon, they completely dismantled my riding mower and put it back together. We all had grease up to our elbows.

Both widowers made tiny but incremental steps toward removing their 'Coats' over the next six months. My demeanor as the unfortunate widow whose husband had left her with a multitude of home repair tasks helped them remember how good it felt to help a woman. My list varied from simple tasks like changing light bulbs that required a ladder, to clearing out tree branches that were hanging over the mower path. I demonstrated my appreciation by making them big pots of soup. All three of us became a little less needy with this simple unspoken arrangement.

As we moved from strangers to friends over the next year, their angry widower parkas came off. One took a job driving widows to doctor appointments, and the other joined a golf league and met a lady who liked to golf. My 'Help Me Coat' turned into a Work Shirt as I learned how to do more home repairs on my own. I actually power washed the driveway and then skim coated the pitted areas with patching cement…a noble task for a 60-something female.

The important thing to understand is that all of us will face adjustments at one time or another. How we handle those adjustments will help us move forward in a positive way. In plain language, widows can feel confused, lonely, angry, fearful, depressed, or desperate. If we can learn that those are normal reactions initially, we can also begin to realize that the pain and negative emotions do not need to last forever. Good books, professional counselling and support groups often help.

My friend, Elaine, shared powerful advice that she received from her husband before he passed. When he realized that he was not going to be able to recover his health, he lovingly told her, "After I die, you should look at it as a new beginning for yourself!" He was a very wise man! His permission to move forward helped her greatly.

Chapter 6

Sometimes There Is No 'Coat' That Helps

Every widow should have an 'Andrea'. She called me regularly twice a week with the sole purpose of easing me away from the 'snake pits' and around the 'boulders' on my trek down the 'widowhood road'. Our friendship started many years before Dean became sick. Although the younger of the two, Andrea seemed to have a calmer approach to life dramas than I did. During each of Dean's LBD crises, Andrea offered poignant bits of advice:

"Remember, your life is perfect for you right now."

"Things are unfolding as they should."

"The things that you have no control over will fall into place."

"Concentrate on the things you can do something about."

"You are, today, the result of the decisions you made yesterday. Consequentially, if you want more peace and prosperity next week, you need to make God-directed choices today."

Andrea's definition of a God-directed choice would be one based on the Golden Rule: "Do to others as you would have them do to you." She made difficult choices seem simple.

Maybe that was the result of becoming a widow at the age of 28. Andrea's first husband, Gary, was only 30 years of age when he developed the brain tumor. They had two small children and little savings left when he passed. Over the years, she turned her expertise as a teacher into a highly-acclaimed career as a Master Teacher, speaking to school groups all over the country. Andrea lived out her tragedy in a way that taught her boys to overcome whatever befalls them. What an example of forging a dynamic new beginning she has been for me!

Hearing the horrific stories Andrea told me about fighting for pension monies and health insurance were jaw-dropping for me until I had to get a lawyer for my own financial problems. The month after Dean died, I quickly learned that there is no 'Coat' to protect a naive woman when society itself minimizes her worth and needs. Figuring out Dean's social security benefits should have been easy. At least that is what the first two clerks told me on the phone before Dean passed. I expected either my own monthly benefit to continue, or elect to receive Dean's continuing monthly amount if it was higher than mine. That would be manageable.

Anything easy disappeared when I sat down in front of the callus man who disputed everything I had been previously told. I had worked for 35 years under my own SSA number, but not in high paying jobs. When the children started in school, I took a job in the school district and collected State Teachers Retirement Funds (STRS) for fifteen years. According to the SSA Man, my authorized SSA benefits had to be penalized because I had collected lump-sum monies when I left the school plan. Hiring an attorney proved futile. He actually gave my initial deposit back to me because he said he learned something he did not previously know. His wife would someday be in the same situation!

Andrea's advice to become familiar with all Dean's death and retirement plans was excellent. What a blessing that Dean had had the wisdom to maintain a small but readily available savings account that I could close out the day before he passed. Without those funds, I would have had no money to pay any bills for 4 months. During my struggle with SSA, I received no social security checks. Using mathematical gymnastics, the government stripped money from both my normal amount and deducted from Dean's monthly amount to allow me about $400 less than I had budgeted. And that was the paper prediction. The powers at SSA also determined that I had been given $7000 too much the year before. I was speechless when I received the letter informing me that I would not receive any checks until that $7000 debt to the government was rectified. Without Dean's wonderful savings, I would have been without any of our social security money until mid-summer…nine months from Dean's passing.

When I could act without yelling, I took the money out of savings and paid the final amount due. As I did so two definitive thoughts surfaced.

First: Widows can't be naive. Others will be out to get their money.

Second: I was old enough to remember that NO GOVERNMENT AGENCY CONTRIBUTED ANY MONEY INTO OUR RETIREMENT ACCOUNTS! It was money that Dean and I had worked to acquire over 50 years! This was a classic example of the government saying, "What's yours is ours!"

The more I talked to Andrea and other widows, the more I realized the financial quagmires that a new widow might face. Not only did Andrea have to fight for Gary's full pension and health plan to be able to care for her two little boys, she had to defer to the rules about remarrying. If she had chosen to marry Barry before all of Gary's benefits could be assured, she would have lost all of Gary's company benefits. Shockingly, Andrea and Barry dated for 15 years before they were finally able to get married. Maybe her fight with the Fire and Policemen's Fund managers helped to make that practice against the law in subsequent years. Public officials are no longer allowed to take retirement benefits away from a widow who remarries…at least in some cities.

Some big companies and municipalities have still been cancelling pensions within the past ten years. My friends, Diane and Edie, experienced that dilemma after their husbands passed. Diane's husband was a government official. She had to get a special ruling from her late husband's civil representative to allow her to keep his pension when she remarried her widower friend. It took her years to secure that decision.

Edie realized she couldn't fight a mega-company. Her best answer was a pledge-commitment to Darrell without legal marriage status. If she had chosen to remarry rather than living with him, she would have lost all her retirement benefits. It was so frustrating for Edie to be forced to lie about making a commitment to a new partner. The older generation has been programmed to believe to do so would be to "live in sin" in the eyes of their families and faith.

Edie and Darrell thoroughly discussed it before deciding to cohabitate. Their research on the financial complications of second marriages was very enlightening.

"Judy, you may find someone new to love," Edie told me.

"That does not seem very probable. I become nauseated if a man hugs me in church."

"Just in case, let me tell you what I learned. If Darrell and I marry, I will lose much of my pension from Stuart's company. I will also lose my health insurance, and it is a good one. Darrell is a good man, but when he was forced to take a medical layoff two years ago, he accumulated a stack of bills. If we get married, I would be responsible for his debts. If he has another heart attack, I would need to pay his medical bills. It is one thing to agree to be his partner and potential caregiver. It is another to volunteer to do that with no money and poor insurance."

"What do your kids think?" I asked Edie.

"The girls are fine with it. They know how much he loves me and wants to make me happy. Both his and my grandkids are thrilled with the attention we show them. My problem is Matt. He thinks Darrell is trying to replace his dad. I hope he can get past that. It is ironic that a big reason for us living in our 'Silver Sin', as Matt labels it, is because we don't want to jeopardize the inheritances for our kids. Stuart left me with a nice nest egg that I hope to leave for my grandkids' college needs. Darrell has an antique car, the farm, and his house. Those things would benefit his children and grandchildren."

I volunteered, "It is infuriating! Whatever happened to America's mandate to take care of the widows and orphans? The greed and bias start with our own government. Because of my social security payout fiasco, I need to go back to work. I start next week."

"That is a perfect example of why both widows and widowers need to have a good attorney to help them avoid the vipers waiting to prey on their resources," Edie replied.

Edie added, "It isn't a pretty situation for baby boomers right now. Everyone seems to be grabbing at our wallets. Just don't give up on finding love again. It is good for the soul."

God, I know that I can say anything to You and You will still love me. This may sound stupid, but I am not sure advancements in society have done anything for the state of widowhood in America. Seriously, God! Could You not have planned a little more charity for the modern-day widow or widower? Societies way of putting a new widow back together is unfair. The "till death-do-you-part" contract didn't specify what happens after the "parted" phase of the contract kicks in.

Maybe a better social system is plural marriages. That was a common custom in Biblical times. There is something to be said for a bevy of wives to take shifts getting through a rough night. Certainly, two widows of the same husband could go out to a restaurant and not be so conspicuous. They could sit up and ask each other the difficult questions at 1:00 in the morning. "Why us? What now?"

I think I have ranted long enough. I do know that many churches provide free income tax preparation for widows. Senior centers offer caregiving and widow support classes. Hospice had a class on getting beyond the grief that I could have attended. My financial planner told me that he had taken the 12-week support classes and found them very helpful.

Perhaps the most important lesson I can offer is for each widow to become a mentor to another new widow. Both can gain from the interaction. The seasoned widow can share what she has learned and feel hope for how far she has come. The new widow can gain from the experiences offered by the other.

Some churches have a walk-beside program that pairs two seasoned widows with a new widow for a year. It provides support and guidance during the early days. In the beginning, every little fact is important. No questions are trivial. As an example, I was energized the first November when I realized that grocery stores offer pumpkin pie in a 1-piece plastic container shaped like a pie wedge at Thanksgiving. I didn't have to go without or buy the whole pie!

Always interested in your inspirations, Lord.

Hi Child,

Anger is natural and healthy. You can vent on Me anytime. That's My job, Little One. You will figure this phase of your life out sooner than you think. It is a necessary process. Better to let all those negative emotions out, or they will eat you up inside. I have very big shoulders; just let Me have them all.

Sleep well. Your Friendly Comforter,

Chapter 7

Redefining Fun

Work hard-play hard was the philosophy Dean and I followed in our family life. We didn't spend much money on alcohol, cigarettes, or exotic food. Our budget centered on sports activities we could do together or as a family. Tennis was the top expenditure after necessities. For years we played in a competitive Friday night league. I remember being so proud of Dean's demeanor with newbie tennis couples. He would play to the caliber of the opponents and take speed and spin out of his shots to make it more competitive. After winning the first set, Dean would say, "How about changing partners, I love to play against my wife." It made for a fun evening for everyone!

As the kids grew, their sports became a family endeavor. Until high school, Dean coached several of their teams alone, or with me as the assistant. That proved fun.

When Dean was a child, his parents took him to almost all of the 50 states. As an adult, he shared his love of traveling with me and the kids. When we became empty-nesters, we thoroughly enjoyed our cruising trips. Those memories were so sharp that I suspected my cruising days might be over forever.

Dean taught me to create fun, to laugh, and to cherish family. When he passed, those avenues for memory-making also stopped. I still had family, but without Dean, the dynamics drastically changed. When visiting my children, I was expected to fit into their worlds, and assume the role of grandparent. For the first two years, neither adult child seemed to understand any of the changes I was forced to accept. To preserve harmony, I accommodated to their routines: I had been where they were; they had never been where I was. It was easier to make the adjustment than to try to explain to them that my world had turned upside-down.

Nothing about tennis was thrilling post-Dean. Mixed doubles required a man and a woman. When no dashing superstar claimed me as a partner, the doors for mixed doubles closed. I no longer felt comfortable socializing at tennis parties. Maybe it was too painful for other wives to see me: "One day that will be me!" Maybe they feared their husbands would prefer me as a partner, which would definitely cause problems. Playing with all women continued, but it did not represent 'fun' as much as a sense that I was *enduring*. Each time I walked off the court, I was grateful to be sufficiently able to walk off the court. Whatever! That door marked "Tennis Fun" was temporarily sealed shut.

Other widows have shared similar stories. Any activity that was shared as a couple became painful for a period: golfing, long walks, neighborhood parties, or even playing card games. Going to places where the attenders are mainly couples is extremely difficult. For many, it is easier to quit the home church than to enter and sit as a single. One friend told me that she had to change grocery stores because she and her husband had always shopped together in one particular store every week. Her shopping was no longer fun.

Forced to make changes, I looked to my friends as role models. Edie's motto was, "Don't ask me to join you if you don't want me to come." She traveled all over Australia with her in-laws. Another friend began traveling on Road Scholar tours (the not-for-profit leader in educational travel) that provided small group interactions. She found that the educational format of those trips took her mind off of herself.

Some of my widow friends were not intimidated when eating alone in a restaurant as I was. They suggested that I stop associating restaurants with dating and start thinking of restaurants as places with fine dining and good food. That helped. I didn't have answers, but I was sure I would recognize 'fun' if it ever returned from where ever it had gone.

Dear God, I realized today that I have made some big changes. Specifically, there is something worse than eating alone in a restaurant, and that would be participating in Diane's Widows Group again. Diane called to invite me to participate as soon as she heard about Dean. I finally agreed, for the Christmas party in her home, my second Christmas as a widow. It was a relatively comfortable and pleasant evening, with both men and women present.

The January Restaurant Night was a different matter. At that gathering, there were 14 women, many with sad, downcast eyes. Generally, I don't judge people by their age, but most of the women in this group were 'old'. The group appeared lifeless, conversation stilted. There was no apparent zest for anything. Diane introduced me as a person who had published a book about my caregiving experiences with my husband. Without a moment's hesitation, the woman across from me emphatically stated, "We could all have written THAT book," abruptly ending any discussion about me or the book. I was thinking, but did not say, "You could have, but I did."

Nothing I could have said would have changed her negative attitude as I realized later in the evening when I threw out an innocent question. "Does anyone have a mixed church group that does fun things together, like going out to ballgames or organizing game nights?" Again, the lady across from me blurted out, "Oh, we know what she's looking for. She wants a man! She wants to get *married*!" It felt like an accusation and a betrayal all rolled into one. I had somehow violated a code of widowhood that I had not been aware existed.

The gentle soul, sitting next to me, raised her eyes and wistfully mentioned that she fully expected to marry again after her husband passed...but it had not happened. I asked her how long he had been gone.

She responded, "Seventeen years."

Whether accurate or not, I got the distinct impression that for this group, the label "unfortunate widow" was branded on my forehead, and I needed to be content with that status for the rest of my life. To expect fun or lively discussions was unacceptable. It made me think about the behavior of lobsters. If one lobster is put into a cage, it will do anything to get out. If two or more lobsters are put into the same cage, the others will attack any lobster trying to escape, literally pulling the defector back into their cage of death.

At first, God, I was angry with this group of women for their lack of compassion and their insensitivity to a fellow sister in pain. The next day, I realized that I had been given a gift. If I didn't do something very different from my present actions, I might become one of the sad-faced lobsters afraid to challenge the hostile leader of the cage. That evening in that restaurant became a mighty motivator to get my mind in shape. The man that loved me unconditionally was gone and not coming back! I needed to step out in faith, believing that something in my future would be good…maybe better than what I had lost.

Nice story, Child. You are making progress,

In the next year, I went to England by myself to meet up with a group of distant cousins on a genealogy excursion. The success of that trip set the pattern for other vacations. Over the next years, I organized work/visit vacations in cities where I had family or friends residing. Once I had the time scheduled with the family or friends, I would rent a condo and arrange book signings with groups before and after the vacation days. This arrangement provided me the luxury of visiting with the cherished people in my life while allowing me the autonomy to promote my book. Traveling became fun again.

Other simple opportunities became fun if I made some simple mental changes:

I enjoyed going to a movie if I went by myself or with another widow. I didn't have to feel guilty about refusing an invitation from Dean's friends to go with them. Although very nice people, the evening became a sad reminder of the past.

I could drive to visit my brother if I listened to books on tape during the long drive.

I could go to group gatherings at church or in the neighborhood, if I drove myself.

I could stay as long as I was comfortable and leave freely when it was no longer fun.

I bought a new tennis racquet and organized a weekly game with three other friends who were also on their own.

In summary, I learned to accept that fun was what I chose for it to be, not what others thought I needed. Besides spending time with family and comfortable friends, it was ok to learn and do new activities.

Chapter 8

'Coats' Come Off, Should Rings?

I was really excited when Andrea and Barry asked if I wanted to go on vacation with them the first summer of my widowhood. We would combine forces: my timeshare condo with their agenda planning. They chose a region that had lots of diverse tourist options: a day of bicycling along a river, several antebellum homes to tour, an art museum, local summer theater, a canoeing trip, and many great restaurants.

When Barry gave me an update the week before the trip, I panicked. Being a caregiver had done a job on my reserves. Regularly playing tennis was not rehabilitating me mentally or emotionally. For the first time in my life, I felt old and ugly. The 20 pounds I had gained feeding Dean six meals a day wasn't coming off easily. I told Barry that I didn't think I had the stamina to do more than one activity a day.

Surprisingly the activities he had planned for day one and two of the trip went well. Stamina didn't present a problem; my attitude did. I wasn't very good company. On the third morning while driving to our first activity, I lamented to Andrea, "I am short-tempered and angry all the time. The grief phase is 90% over. That is not the issue. I started the grieving process two years before Dean died when I realized that he wasn't going to get better. I have been doing well until recently. Now everything bugs me: people, traffic lights that won't change, yappy dogs. Nothing seems to be going right."

"Take off the ring! You are not married anymore. You won't get past thinking that he is out visiting his mother until you quit wearing your wedding ring on your left hand," Andrea responded without even taking a deep breath.

Wham! Bam! I was so surprised that I lurched backward in the car seat as if Andrea had slapped me along-side of the head with a big stick.

"I can't do that! I had my diamond reset before Dean got sick, and I like it. It is my 'Forever Ring.' What does wearing my diamond have to do with my crankiness? You are goofy!" I responded with irritation in my voice.

"Your choice, but until you take off the ring, your mind is still telling you that things haven't changed, 'You are still married.' Obviously, that is not the case, and you are frustrated. At least take it off your left hand and wear it on your right hand. I can tell you for sure that no man will even talk to you with that ring on your finger."

"That makes no sense, and I am certainly not interested in finding anyone to date," I insisted.

"Well, humor me and at least think about it."

I did think about it all day. I went from being absolutely convinced that Andrea was crazy, to playing with it on my finger, to actually taking it off and putting it on the right third finger.

The next day when we got into the car to go to breakfast, I thrust my right hand forward over the front seat and said, "There, it is on my right hand!" Andrea just smiled and didn't say a word.

Amazingly, that day was really fun. I was energetic, displayed a sense of humor, and felt new thoughts and ideas running through my mind. Life was good! As the day progressed, I leaned back in the seat and admitted, "I have had a great time making memories today...something I was not sure would ever happen again."

Although my attitude had changed dramatically after I switched the diamond from my left hand to my right hand, I did not attribute any change in my mood to the ring switch. Until that evening...

At the last minute, the three of us agreed to attend the summer theater if we could get tickets. Barry was able to get the last three available tickets and handed me mine: the second seat in the top row of four seats. Shortly after we sat down, a nice-looking gentleman my age sat down next to me. A conversation began and became interesting quickly. We talked during the entire evening as if we were long lost friends. I was struck with how easy it was to have a pleasant conversation with a total stranger. He had been a widower for about two years. As we compared notes, I was amazed at the similarities of our emergence from the feelings of grief to yearnings for more out of life. He apparently had moved along the road farther than I had because he told me that he had fallen in love with a very special lady and was intending to spend the rest of his life with her. Their wedding was scheduled for the next March.

After the performance, Barry suggested that we stop for a dessert at a corner restaurant. He and Andrea could barely contain their merriment that I had been talking to a MAN all evening. For them, the ring switch opened up the universe to an adventure; and I had been gifted with a good one.

That night as I lay in my bed, reliving the conversation, I determined to keep the ring on my Right hand, just in case Andrea was right. Then I had to smile as I realized that my new friend had managed to climb out of his lobster cage. Good for him!

I was profoundly grateful to have a smart, dedicated friend willing to share a complicated but necessary piece of wisdom. I felt blessed knowing that not everyone has a guide like that. If the 14 ladies in Diane's Widows Group had had an 'Andrea', maybe they would have moved their wedding rings to their right hands. Who knows what kind of stimulating adventures they might have had?

As for me that week, I exchanged my 'Coats' of Widowhood for a bicycle helmet, sightseeing sneakers, and a canoeing life jacket. Being on that vacation with Andrea and Barry helped shape my willingness to step out with faith that something in the unknown might become a really good experience.

Chapter 9

Love Is Better Than A 'Coat'

2012
More Reflections on the First Years of My Widowhood

One Sunday in that first December after Dean passed, I wandered the mall to buy Christmas gifts for the grandchildren. When I had pulled into the mall garage, I was apprehensive that I might feel too sad to shop. Surprisingly, to be able to meander by myself through the stores with no time constraints and no one to wonder where I was, gave me a strange sense of joy. Time seemed to stand still as I savored the decorations, music and Christmas pageantry everywhere, allowing the euphoria of unbridled freedom. Dean was safe now with no danger of falling and breaking a hip. He had completed his journey and done his illness to the best of his ability. It was over!

Shopping this Christmas was different because I was alone. Yet reminiscing about our many other shopping trips together, made this afternoon feel like Dean was walking by my side. Several hours of aimlessly meandering, found me sitting at the diamond counter in our favorite jewelry store…talking to a salesperson about post earrings. Dean had taken me on a shopping adventure each of the past several years until he became too ill. It had become our annual hunting expedition. The salesperson would pull out several post diamonds, and I would ogle, but never score a final selection.

Surprisingly, this particular afternoon, I found the perfect earrings; precisely what I had pictured in my imagination all those prior years. Finding the perfect earrings on this specific adventure seemed like a God-Moment. Unlike my normal routine of looking first at the price tag, the cost for these stones was irrelevant. The whole afternoon had been almost surreal. I bought the diamonds on the spot and wore them home.

Looking back over the first year of my widowhood, those earrings on that Christmas shopping trip seemed to be Dean's loving way of telling me that I deserved them. They were a tangible Christmas hug from him, and I was okay with that. I found it interesting that when I stopped wearing my diamond ring on my left finger that next summer, I felt no need to remove the post earrings. In fact, I wore the earrings for two more years. They never came out of my ears. It was almost as if Dean was saying to me "You are becoming a new you; you need new beautiful diamonds to celebrate that process."

Hello God,

I bet that You thought I forgot to come and talk to You. After all, this is the first letter to You in the past year. I know You are near; I feel Your presence in many little ways.

I have been trying to make sense by reflecting rather than writing. This year, being alone has helped me understand the great importance of feeling loved. I think I took Dean's love for granted all our years together. Now I realize that it was the thing I never doubted. I felt reasonably complete with his love always present in my life during the good times and the bad. If I had to describe the 'Me' this year without him, it might be a lump of Swiss cheese filled with holes. Maybe a better analogy would be Charlie, the ugly little puppy I found the summer adventure in California before I went to graduate school. He was such a forlorn, scraggy little creature. Someone had left him to fend for himself, and he wasn't faring very well. I almost killed him when I turned the hose water on him to wash away the bugs. After I flew him home with me to Wisconsin, he thrived on the love that my parents and I showered upon him. That love made him feel secure. He knew that we didn't care what he looked like.

At this stage of my widowhood journey, I understand that I need to find another source of unconditional love. Through my parenting years, I presumed that the logical place to put my love would be onto my kids, but they can't give back what I am looking for.

AJ is a great comfort. He has been a good son and has tried very hard to make me feel worthwhile. But he lives five hours away. The love I need must reflect a genuine appreciation for who I am today and for all I will become. Judy Towne Jennings is a work in progress right now.

Hello, Child,

So, what is new? Here I am telling you that you are on the right path and all will work out in its proper timing. This is just part of the same old talk we have had for many years. Be patient, Little Flower, you will have your answers. You will know who you are and why you are here, for your work is not yet done. Your teaching will begin soon

As far as Love is concerned...don't try so hard to minimize the pain of loss you have experienced. The pain will strengthen you into a better person if you can overcome the bitterness surrounding it. You are doing well with Dean's passing... not so much with the reactions of others. You might respond to those who have pulled away as if they too had developed a disease. Guard against anger. Unleashed, it will confine you and not allow you to grow.

So, Dear Child, find a sense of grace for any hurtful exchanges you experienced during

Dean's sickness and passing. Many others also grieved for him, and grief can be an alienating companion. Compassion with forbearance freely given will serve you best. If you want some kind of change, remember, you can only change yourself.

That brings Me to your search for love. You can't find a source of real genuine love until you are ready to open your heart and let it in. Your cave dwelling attitude is a pretty good indication that you are not prepared to open up to receive the love that is even similar to what you had with Dean. You will know when you don't mind missing your sacred episodes of TV programs. They are safe right now, and safe is good.

Be gentle with yourself. When you said that the love you need is a true appreciation for who you are today, you are more accurate than you yet realize. One day you will understand that you must first love yourself unconditionally before you will have an abundance of love to give to another. You have more lessons to learn, but all in good time. Reread your "Desiderata". I gave it to you those many years ago, just for times such as these.

It is okay to write to Me more often than once a year. I do know what I am talking about. I am the incredible source of wisdom tucked away in your computer, after all.

Sleep tight.

Your loving friend

"DESIDERATA"

Go placidly amid the noise and haste, and remember what peace there may be in silence. As far as possible, without surrender, be on good terms with all persons. Speak your truth quietly and clearly; and listen to others, even the dull and ignorant; they too have their story.

Avoid loud and aggressive persons, they are vexations to the spirit. If you compare yourself with others, you may become vain and bitter; for always there will be greater and lesser persons than yourself. Enjoy your achievements as well as your plans.

Keep interested in your own career, however humble; it is a real possession in the changing fortunes of time. Exercise caution in your business affairs; for the world is full of trickery. But let this not blind you to what virtue there is; many persons strive for high ideals, and everywhere life is full of heroism.

Be yourself. Especially, do not feign affection. Neither be cynical about love; for in the face of all aridity and disenchantment, it is perennial as the grass.

Take kindly the counsel of the years, gracefully surrendering the things of youth. Nurture strength of spirit to shield you in sudden misfortune. But do not distress yourself with imaginings. Many fears are born of fatigue and loneliness. Beyond a wholesome discipline, be gentle with yourself.

You are a child of the universe, no less than the trees and the stars; you have a right to be here. And whether or not it is clear to you, no doubt the universe is unfolding as it should.

Therefore, be at peace with God, whatever you conceive Him to be, and whatever your labors and aspirations, in the noisy confusion of life keep peace with your soul.

With all its sham, drudgery and broken dreams, it is still a beautiful world. Be careful. Strive to be happy.

Found in Old Saint Paul's Church, Boston, Massachusetts
Written by Max Erhmann, 1927, Terre Haute, Indiana
Copyright: public domain

Chapter 10

Letters

2012
Reflections of the First Two Years of Widowhood

Reflecting on my own experience since Dean's passing two years earlier was easier to do when I would write. It became my personal mode of defusing an internal tornado. My friends handled their widowhood in various ways: going back to work, volunteering for Meals on Wheels, or babysitting their grandchildren full time. There is no one-size-fits-all for overcoming grief. Pain is a great motivator to find acceptable ways to be meaningful. My letters to God evidenced my transitional journey from being a broken widow to becoming an authentic woman who happened to be widowed.

Finding meaning and comfort through my writings started after my mother passed in 1987. My writing dialogues with my mom became almost as significant as our phone conversations had been when Mom was in California and I was in Ohio. The tone of her words in my thoughts was the 'Her' when she was alive. Whether discussing what life in Heaven was like or chastising me for being grumpy with the kids, I felt that the words were spiritually driven, and proved very comforting.

I reflected, "I certainly never anticipated that writing letters and receiving responses from the loving spirits filling the spaces around me would allow me to have the friendly adventures over the years that I now claim. Supernatural phenomena can be helpful when centered in a love for God with all my heart, soul and mind, and a love for my neighbor as myself."

Dear God,

I am not sure what I would have done if I hadn't had You living in my computer readily accessible these past few years. Putting my thoughts on paper, whether ugly or happy, seems to center me. Maybe if my mom were still alive, I would still be venting to her. I envy other women who have a close relationship with a sister or living parent.

I have such a firm belief in our 'friendship' now that I want others to experience the peace, joy, and human validation writing to You has given to me. I don't think I am weird or an exception, and I don't believe You are a figment of my imagination. The words that surface after I ask for Your response are too diverse from my own usual way of looking at events, to not accept a divine nature to the counsel that Your letters have provided to me.

Love, J

Dear J,

So, true. You are accurate in thinking that not everyone will access this communication style that we have. I tend to meet people where they are. This just happens to work for us. But you are also accurate in thinking that it can work for others who want to have this seek and find inspired adventure, meditating by writing into a computer.

Thanks for sharing

Dear God,

I like the letter we shared some years ago when You suggested that I should begin to 'converse' with my mother again. Once I started my messages with You, I wasn't sure I should be talking to anyone but You. After receiving this letter, I assumed that if it is okay to talk to Mom, and also later to Dean after he passed.

Letters to God and Mom: Good Friday 2003, and First Easter after Dean Passed, 2011.

2003

My dear child,
You are trying to listen, but your heart is heavy. You know that negative feelings invite the dark elements. I have freed you from your anger. Work hard to keep yourself clear. You will hear My message so much clearer without the clouds of negativity garbling up the space between us. If you can stay clear, you will also not eat so much. You are not really hungry. You are missing your unconditional love source, your mother. You have a void to fill. Don't use food. You will have a cycle of self-loathing if you get heavy. You have been there before. Might as well go back to talking to your mother. She is, after all, My messenger, a piece of Myself, a drop from My ocean. She will not lead you astray. She is the person meant just for you, to show you My unconditional love in person. And what you learn from her will directly apply to your relationship with your children. Go write to your Mother.

Example of a Letter to My Mom, Good Friday 2003

Hi Mom,
Guess I haven't written in a while. How is it going where you are? It is almost Easter when we have usually had our annual talk. It was a convenience for me that you passed on Good Friday. Helps me reminisce every Good Friday and make time to sit with you.

Hello Dear,

We can talk more than once a year you know. But I know you are busy, so I don't barge in very often. On occasion, I "whisper" in your ear. I am glad you are back into the genealogy research. There are lots of beneficial messages there for you. We come from good people.

I know you are frustrated with how your life is going right now, all the Physical Therapy challenges, Dean's lack of strength, aches, and pains. Your difficulties are not something you can share easily with your kids. They have their own path direction right now with their individual lessons. Old age complaints fall better on ears that can understand that it is just rambling and venting. Not meant to be acted upon. If you tell your kids about your aging complaints, they think they have to fix something to ease your burden. And THEY can't. We have to carry our own loads. That is all I was doing all those times when you came complaining to me about Dean not doing this or that. Just reminding you that you had to carry your own load. Usually worked. You are still together.

It is natural for me to talk to you. But others think it is strange. Do you also talk to Brother?

I talk to him more than you think. He listens. You know there are many of us here who look after you all. But be assured, things are progressing as they should. You are all good people, with good hearts. Have a nice spring, Dear. I know you like this time of year. I do too.

Love you, Mom

The First Talk with Dean the First Easter after He Had Passed, 2011

How does one converse with a departed husband? It was hard enough to get him to have a heart to heart when he was living here on earth. But learning to direct my thoughts toward God made it easy to imagine that

I was talking to Dean. I put one of Dean's pictures in a chair facing outward. I sat on the ottoman in front of the picture and told him anything I could think of to tell him. Then I just cleared my mind, closed my eyes, and waited. It seemed like a long wait. And then I heard thoughts in my head that sounded like something Dean might say.

"What's up? I'm here. Got to get the hang of how to do this."

"Hi, Sweetie! What is it like there? Do you see Mom?" (doubting this whole occurrence.)

"Oh yeah, all the time," he replied.

"Do you see your parents?"

"Everyone, for generations back. There are multitudes of people here."

"How does this work? Can you always see me and everything on earth?" I asked.

"No, I can only be with you if you open your heart to me. If you stop loving me, I'll be gone."

"Interesting. Can you be with AJ or the grandkids?" I asked.

"AJ has carved out a good place for himself. He needs a strong woman with great business skills. Caryn is that. He loves her and their life. I'm proud of the direction he has chosen. There were times I was worried about how he would make it with all his anger. As it is, he feels blessed and responds with more patience and kindness than I thought he would show. I'm pleased for him."

"What about politics?"

"Oh boy. I'm glad I'm here. The infighting is pretty strong. It really doesn't weigh on me much anymore. What will be will be...part of the history of the world. Not a big issue in the grand scheme of things. As long as you are there, you need to fight for right and justice. Do what you can. Get involved. Be Bold."

"If you have any inspirations for me as Mom does… can you whisper in my ear?" I asked.

"No, you know that is not my style. I wish I could; I watch and admire you. I send you memories now and then. I can read your letters if you ask, and give you suggestions like I used to do. Call me in before you push send."

"What do you think of the book that I am working on?"

"It is fine that you are writing it. If you can make a few pennies, go for it. Was nice to see all the love you are putting into it, but nobody will read it."

"WHAT? I CAN'T BELIEVE YOU FEEL THAT WAY," I exploded.

"People won't care about my story. They will be interested in their own life."

"Well, this is interesting. I can't believe I am sitting here angry at a dead guy."

"If it sells, it will be because of your writing, not how I lived with a disease."

"Any other thoughts?" I queried as I smiled at our interchange.

"You have people around you that care about you. That is good. I don't worry about you."

"I will keep my heart open. I loved the way you loved me – unconditionally," I responded.

"That was my job. Have a good week. Love you."

"Love you too, Dean."

2011
April

Letters worked for me. Spending time in quiet dialogue with people who had loved me unconditionally helped me appreciate that I was still lovable. It also forced me to see myself with a sense of humor and a sense of humility.

"I certainly do not have all the answers to the workings of the Universe! I am conversing, after all, with my deceased relatives. What does that mean? "

To feel loved was an essential aspect of healing, but I reasoned that only God could know what else could improve my focus and purpose.

Chapter 11

New Lessons Begin

2011
September

I could not write during Dean's last summer until well into the next year. Putting ideas in letters during the early years of the disease had been cathartic as if pulling porcupine quills out of an attacked part of the body. In the center of the Valley of Death and Tunnel of Grief, all I could do was survive. It took almost a year before I was able to look at my journal files again. Organizing them into a format kept me busy and seemed to lessen my grief.

In the summer before the anniversary of Dean's passing in October, I saw a book-publishing offer in my emails specifically for first-time authors. A publisher of Christian books had released the announcement of a contest awarding five authors with a free book publishing contract. The book submission deadline was January 31, 2012. I had never seen any email advertising book publishing before this one, but little things like logic had never stopped God's apparent promptings before. He always seemed to have His ways of motivating me.

You have been very good at embracing the messages I have sent to you. Most people have

not yet learned that I do work directly in their lives, every day. A message is always the strongest if one can hear it when one is in a situation where one really needs it. Unfortunately, too many people assume there is no message coming and turn away in frustration. The hardest task is seeing a sign where it is least expected. The Bible is not always My vehicle of choice. But then, I can reverse the poles on the earth. I am able to do My work MY Way.

You are ready for new lessons. It is time for you to organize your caregiving journal. Tell your story. You need to put it on paper, not only for you but for others.

The fire had been lit with the advertisement to write a book. Over the next two months, I put all my caregiving experiences into a book format. Evidently, my work was found worthy because as the first draft was finished, an editor was dropped into my life...

In late September, a friend called to tell me she had found a boyfriend for me, and she wanted me to come to a house party that next Sunday to meet Bob. As an incentive, she added that he edited books.

I went and met Bob. He was much more important than a boyfriend. He was a perfect editor and became fully invested in completing my book by mid-January. It was the right time in his life to edit again after a long hiatus. More precisely, he had had to stop working to become a caregiver for an unmarried aunt until she passed. There would have been no book without Bob's sharp purging, clarifying, and comma insertions. Bob was an answer to a prayer that I didn't even know I needed to pray.

The book was submitted but did not win. Of more importance to me was a new budding belief that since I had, indeed, written the manuscript for a book, I was only one step away from being an author. With my contestant discount, my (God's inspired) book was printed and ready for marketing in September of 2012. I had listened and put my lessons onto paper. As I held a copy of my finished book, it was irrelevant whether anyone would find it helpful. It had accomplished a restoration in me that completely changed my purpose in life!

Letter I Wrote to Myself After the Book was Published in 2012

This October of 2012, two years after Dean's passing, I have a sense of who I am as a single person. Most of the negatives are behind me. I don't know how the future will unfold, but I am enthusiastic and ready to embark in new directions. I have a God-given task to tell people about our adventure during Dean's illness and passing.

My speaking career about caregiving is launched, and I have been asked to write articles for caregiving magazines. Because of divine inspiration with dependable help when needed, my life has completely turned around. Literally out of the ashes of our destroyed married life, I have a new career and an important reason to be alive.

I realize that when a widow can embrace change, there is hope for a new life chapter to begin. A powerful dream involving Dean showed me that I am heading in a new direction and it will be good. It felt that God confirmed that in His response to my musing.

Dear God,

Thank You for the dream last night. In it, I had a wonderful, and powerfully intimate reunion with Dean. I have never had anything of that nature before. In fact, I haven't dreamed about Dean very often for over a year.

This morning I pondered the message of that dream and recorded it in my dream notebook to be sure I remembered all the details. These are some of the ideas that the symbolism could be pointing me to consider.

1. I am learning to balance the male and female polarities of myself, merging my individual qualities with Dean's…a blending of our strengths. My mind could have been reflecting on the importance of our partnership during the worst time of our lives, culminating with a finished book about our story together.

2. On a literal level, maybe I just missed my husband.

3. Since I explicitly asked for a sign that You, God, were endorsing my writing and speaking career, I choose to interpret the dream as Your message that life will be on a higher plane. I will reach the mountaintop!

It will be fun to wait and see what happens next. I place it in Your hands, God.

"I have built you for adventures to the top of the mountains. Sometimes you will reach the summit. Other times you will learn skills in the climbing that help with the next mountain adventure. I have your back! Enjoy your enthusiasm today. You have earned it.

Just remember, you are not alone. You are not overworked. You are not abandoned. You are not anything else that signifies a negative. Don't be afraid to embrace the lesson that Pastor Jeff taught you and your youth group when you went camping many years ago. Be willing to say "I am Your beloved child in whom You are well pleased."

Sleep well, My child.

Chapter 12

Godly 'Doings' And
Godly 'Un-Doings'

Spring 2013
Third Year of Widowhood

My story is not unique, but it is the one I know intimately. I tell it because people feel more comfortable if they realize they are not the only ones having problems. Just possibly, the person on the path in front of them might see light at the end of the tunnel.

After the high of publishing my LBD book, I fell into a despondency pit. No longer needing to pour myself into my writing all day allowed reality to surface like an angry foe. This despondency was a cloud I couldn't get out from under. Most people would have remarked that I appeared back to normal. When I would describe my quality of life, I remarked that I had highs and lows. Life wasn't a Hallmark special, but it had improved from a black and white melodrama.

Although I desperately tried, I wasn't getting past the heart pangs everywhere I went: the tennis club, church potlucks, even grocery shopping. Memories were attached to every aspect of life in my little Ohio town. Although seeing my friends with healthy husbands had stopped making me cry, finding one of Dean's business cards tucked into a dresser drawer would produce an avalanche of tears.

During the moments when my deeply buried feelings rose to the surface, I realized I was fighting a battle with frightening 'unknowns'. What would my life look like in a month, a year, ten years? Could I fend on my own? Would I be able to handle my finances? Would I remain alone forever? The powerful 'unknowns' seemed to be winning. Where was that door to Tomorrowland where many new friends were waiting with time to play and a zest for life? What had happened to the exhilaration that I felt when I held my printed book?

I had enjoyed some fame locally with the book in six months and had spoken to many groups. Speaking seemed to be a noble endeavor that always brought me pleasure. People wrote to tell me how pleased they were to hear me and to learn from my experience. Writing the book to honor my husband and our journey, creating a handbook for others to lean into should have given me a sense of purpose and ever-present joy. I had completed my big task and it was a success. I should have cemented my new identity. Why was I continuing to be a shape without distinctive features? How did I fill the voids?

Coincidently, while maneuvering through this dark cloud, a series of physical calamities definitely got my attention. The first occurred when I was power washing my concrete driveway and the phone rang in the garage. I turned off the machine unaware of what can happen to the water pressure in the hose when the pressure is released, I dropped the nozzle and stepped over the hose. Wrong choice! The hose literally jumped up off the ground as I attempted to step over it and grabbed both legs forcing me to do a full out belly flop onto the pavement. I had blood on both elbows and severe pain in both kneecaps.

My initial reaction was to look around to see if anyone had seen my unceremonious fall onto the pavement. I was a tennis player and not accustomed to such an un-grounding. After licking my wounds for a few days, I ignored it.

A full out catastrophe finally got my attention in May. I was on my way to teach at a hospital in Indiana when I stopped at a rest stop. On the way back to the car, my right ankle started to turn for absolutely no physical reason. There was no impediment on the sidewalk. I was not feeling weak or infirm in any way.

To correct my balance, I leaned to the left, but overcorrected and went down hard onto my left hip. My initial thought was that I was embarrassed, and hoped no one had seen my fall. I hopped up and could stand on the leg. That was good. It wasn't broken! I made it the ten yards to my car, got in and then panicked. The pain was severe with any movement of any part of the leg. As long as I was sitting, the pain was tolerable, but my Physical Therapy assessment told me that I would not be able to walk.

After regaining some amount of reason, I elected to continue driving to the hospital. My contact lady had a wheelchair and assistant ready in the hospital garage to meet me. I spoke to her audience from the wheelchair, agreed to have an x-ray of the hip, but chose to drive back home when the x-ray verified that nothing was broken. When I got near home, I called a friend who sent her husband to help. Jocko met me at my driveway with a walker. Without his brute strength, I would never have made it up the two steps in front of my house. Together we managed to get me to the bedroom where I crashed onto my bed. What a crazy experience that day had been!

The pain was excessive for three days and kept me confined to bed except to hobble to the commode with a walker. My daughter and friends provided food.

The hospital emergency department gave no diagnosis. Google and my assessment of the symptoms coincided with the football injury: hip pointer. It took three weeks to be able to walk without the walker and three months before I could again play tennis. (This would not be the usual course of action for someone without medical knowledge. Once I realized no bones were broken, I knew the treatment would be rest and Physical Therapy. I could do all that by myself.)

Finding the real reason for the falls and the pit of despondency was pressing. The next accident could be a broken hip or worse. I had plenty of time as I healed to search for answers. I read several books on grief, anger, anxiety, depression, faith, spiritual warfare, and the connection between the mind and body.

I researched several websites about Anxiety and Depression to get a better explanation of what I had been experiencing. (The Anxiety and

Depression Association of America websites, adaa.org and anxiety.org, had good information.)

Education is always good. Recognizing mental issues is important. Until we know what is keeping us down, we can't take appropriate steps to overcome despair. The most important piece of information to understand is that prolonged anxiety is linked to severe health issues. Cardiac dysfunction is just one of many.

I decided to briefly note some of the information I had learned:

Anxiety is normal in everyday life. Excessive and persistent anxiety over an extended time moves the healthy physiologic mechanisms into the unhealthy zones. Stress triggers normal hormones and enzymes to help a person act to preserve life and limb, "flight or fight". For high alert body organs to work best, other non-essential systems slow down. One of those is the immune system. Pesky coughs can last for months. Examples of two others are proper digestion and sleep functions. A side issue of prolonged stress is inflammation in various parts of the body. Inflammation clogs up the wheels of good health.

I should have remembered all this from the information I had learned moving past the stress damage of caregiving. My weight had topped out, digestion was poor and sleep dysfunctional. My naturopathic doctor had told me that my stress hormone, Cortisol, was excessively high. During that time, the only food I could digest was sugar. Once I cut back on the sugar and took pills to decrease the inflammation in my gut, I lost weight and regained normal health.

Being in a Pit Requires that One Admit To Being in a Pit.

I was shocked to see evidence of an anxiety disorder in my symptoms. Whew! Interesting! I couldn't watch anything on TV except Hallmark movies. If a new book had any chaos for the heroine, I couldn't finish it. My method of passing time was doing jigsaw puzzles on my I-Pad. It was almost as if my mind knew that I was straining to put the pieces of my life together. Completion of a jigsaw puzzle placated any angst for a while.

Guilt, grief, fear, hopelessness crept in for some part of everyday. Some stayed longer than others. The end-result was a need to avoid friends.

My talks with God helped as did prayer but didn't overcome my feelings of pessimism and hopelessness. More frequently, I was finding a lack of interest in things that previously brought joy. At times, my question, "Is this all there is?" was switching to, "This IS all there is! The best part of my life is Over!" When those moments surfaced, I would be unable to think, concentrate, exercise, laugh or talk to anyone. For no reason during some evenings, I realized I wasn't breathing correctly. My chest was constricted, hands clenched, breathing shallow.

Getting to sleep was difficult. On the worst nights, I found I was back to my caregiving anxiety of letting the negative thoughts in my mind cycle like a tape on replay for hours. Many nights, I was awakening with bad dreams. Apparently, I had managed to suppress my grief while writing. When given a chance to surface, it flooded my mind. When my meditations with my computer spiritual counselor had warned me not to hurry through my grieving, He knew what He was advising. Writing had buried my grief prematurely.

As I worked to heal my physical maladies, I had to wonder if there might be a mind/body connection or spiritual warfare acting on my wellbeing. Yes, I was widowed, but I was also elated about teaching and mentoring other caregivers and health care professionals about Lewy Body Dementia. It was as if something vicious was trying to destroy my chance of happiness. Spiritual entities would certainly like to see me fail. And I had to wonder if my own psyche would allow me to be happy and successful.

Enter God

From experiences in my distant past, I should have known that when God was ready for me to learn new life lessons He would intercede. It could be a gentle prod, a dump onto the derriere, or wonderful surprising God-Moments. Some seemed to suspend the rules of the Universe.

Knowing that I was searching for answers, my daughter invited me to attend a Restoring Lives Week-long Conference in September. It provided nuggets of awareness that began to help me restore my health physically, emotionally, mentally, and spiritually.

The conference format recommended that each participant write a letter to God.

This is mine.

I went to the Restoring Lives Conference this week very anxious about what wisdom if any, I might gain for the direction of my life. The bottom line is that I wanted to be healed and to prevent any future illnesses or injuries.

The first nugget I brought home was that sickness and/or injury can be a wake-up call. Mind/body work with You, God, is required to eradicate all my 'Un-wellness'. I must purge my negative thinking and dump the mental garbage I am carrying within every cell in my body: un-forgiveness, bitterness, anger, guilt, and fear. If I can be successful cleaning out my own garbage dump, I might be able to stop sabotaging myself. I have a path in front of me where I can share my experiences and potentially help others. I have skills, but I need to accept the challenges that You have provided for me. I don't need to be perfect or be the best. I do need to trust that You will provide for my needs and never leave me. If I can't overcome all my own negatives and insecurities, I will be a fraud.

I am sure You didn't cause me to fall, but I am also sure that You allowed my own self-destructive tendencies to trip me up. What a humbling awareness that I have allowed my own mind to play havoc with my body. I now realize that I have been carrying a lot of anger and fear. Dean's sickness took me by surprise and I never understood why he needed to die?

During the conference this week, I finally understood that I was allowed to let it go. His dying wasn't because of something we did or didn't do. You are God and I am not. If it was his time to depart, anger at him or You would serve no good.

The fear component surprised me as well. I hadn't realized that I was feeling like Dean and I were being punished, and we didn't even know why. Because I judged that death was a punishment, I was holding on to the fear that I needed to be near perfect to be sure some other loved one wouldn't die or suffer great pain. With the conference explanation of mind/body connections, I was able to enjoy my success and let go of the idea that Death was punitive. I have accepted that I am good enough in Your eyes. And most importantly, I was not responsible for

Dean's dying. But! I am responsible for my own condition, mentally and physically.

The second task that I need to do is to be 'right' with You. That requires making amends with any of Your other children! Ouch. I will apologize to as many people as I can list. I also pledge to forgive anyone who may have hurt me intentionally or unintentionally during Dean's time of sickness. And the flip side is important. If anyone offered help or solace, I pledge to tell them how much I appreciated their effort.

My pride is gone. I must have been doing a lot of wrong thinking to be so violently ungrounded. I will be more tuned in to what Your suggested directions for me might be in the future. I can assure You that You have my attention. I don't ever want another physically painful wake-up call.

I am your obedient, grateful child.

> **Dear Child,**
>
> **Your letter makes me smile. It is truly my plan in action. Free will wins again. Sorry, you had to have the medical discountenances to get your attention. Part of the laws of nature. Negative begets more negative. Sometimes dis-ease is a better teaching tool than the promise of great riches.**
>
> **I am also pleased that you finally have found your destiny. Use the medical calamities in a person's life to alert them to the Mind/Body problems that might really be making them sick. Now that you have lived it, you can better teach it. I am the Great Physician, and only through Me can anyone be fully healed. As you realized, sickness can serve as a flashlight that points the path to ME.**

Why couldn't Dean be made well? We asked for the Angels and a miracle.

> **Dean was made well, spiritually. Once he had the healing, he came back to Me. His mission in**

life was finished. He had accomplished all the work he contracted to do. Dean patiently loved you into a whole person. He was a useful father until he could do no more for your children. He gave you the opportunity to learn from your caregiving. When apparent that he could do more from this side with Me than he could do there, I called him home, and he was happy to come.

It was not his commission to tell the world that sickness can be a mental thing, a soul thing. It is yours. Thank him for his willingness to serve out his duties for you to learn that. He did his job very well. I am pleased.

Go to church. You will be late. We will talk much more as you stay open to all the new things I have yet to teach you.

Your loving triune

My To-Do List for Overcoming Stress

1. Finish something within the next two weeks that has been weighing me down

2. Schedule strenuous exercise 3x/week, some exercise daily
   - Lift weights at least 1x/week
   - Walk

3. Stop all sugar, butter, and desserts
   - Eat protein 3x/day
   - Take my vitamins every day
   - Get a medical check-up annually

4. Add some beauty to my life

- Buy a safer car
- Wear makeup
- Plant flowers
- Make my bed every day

5. Apologize quickly and with sincerity to God and others

6. Say Thank you often to God and others

7. Spend time with people who make me laugh
    - Grandkids

8. Be open to the opportunities to touch another person's life to ease his/her discomforts.

Chapter 13

Mastering Widowhood

2013-2014

By November of 2013, I was back to playing tennis, teaching regularly to groups around Cincinnati and moving out to nearby states for conference talks. Fortunately, I was able to relieve my anxiety with the Restoring Lives work. Life was good. I felt like I had mastered widowhood and was beginning a new chapter of my life with unbounded opportunities available. As a person who processes feelings on paper, I pondered how I had done that.

God was the facilitator for me and would need to be the facilitator for every other widow. In my ponderings, I recognized that all I could do was identify some simple truths that might universally work for anyone after the loss of a loved one. My journey was personal as everyone else's journey would be personal for them. In that, Dean had been correct. Others would be seeking answers to their own difficulties.

But Dean missed the fact that we all need pathfinders, those that take the first steps out of catastrophe, and then the next. He inspired me to write about his acceptance of his disease and his efforts to make every day matter. If I could tell his story with humor, it would be God's way to tell others that help and change are available. Restoring Lives helped me see that allowing my recurring negative thoughts free range, I was effectively sabotaging all my good intentions. Having a structured plan that gives us purpose and joy is the goal.

Acceptance

I didn't ask to be a caregiver or a widow. Once those conditions landed on my plate, I had to make choices: educate myself, survey friends, recognize pitfalls, and make the best of the situation with humor and compassion. But this time, the humor and compassion needed to be directed to heal myself.

Adventure Attitude

As a new public speaker, I had to take a leap of faith that my message could help others dealing with the dementia quagmire. My 'AHA!' moment came as I spoke to a large group of residents and family members at Fair Haven Retirement Complex in Indianapolis. When I was invited by the Activity Director to give the opening message for a wellness conference, it was suggested that I use humor in my talk. I gulped as I realized that this could be a challenge.

There I was standing before 70 people (many who no longer laughed well) talking about how important it was to 'find' one good belly laugh each week. When I related several of my experiences while living with a jokester husband, some of the wives laughed so hard that they bobbed in their seats. I told them about the time Dean turned the shower spray up over the glass doors to thoroughly douse me while I stood by the sink waiting to help him maneuver out of the shower.

"Dean! What are you doing?"

"Oh, did I get you all wet?" he responded gleefully.

"Yes, and the ceiling, pictures, and curtains!"

Those serendipitous moments between us shattered the frustrations governing our lives, if only for a few moments. And humor did that for the audience that afternoon. I had created a comic routine out of the shards of a broken life. Making others laugh was a revelation for me and an adventure for them.

None of my widow friends chose my public speaking path, but those that chose to have adventures did well recreating themselves.

Attitude of Gratitude

I found that it was very difficult to wallow in self-pity when I was commending another person for kindnesses shown. It was also difficult to be grumpy when I was reaching out to help a sister who was entering the role of a caregiver or transitioning to the life of a widow. Both extending gratitude and receiving a 'Thank you' made me a nicer person to be near. Gratitude helped dissolve my prickliness.

Recognizing the Godly interventions during each day became second nature. If I routinely thanked God sincerely for those God Moments, it seemed that I received more of His attention. It is more likely that I trained myself to recognize that God was always with me. I was the one missing His ever-present assistance.

An I-Can Attitude

It might not be easy to start over, but it is do-able. I had to believe that whatever I encountered, I could overcome. At one Christmas dinner in Winchester, I was the motivational speaker for 100 widows, almost all of them over 80 years of age. I did not have that piece of information before I planned my talk. There was no going back when I got to the auditorium. My prepared talk was scraped and I extemporaneously spoke about an I-Can Attitude.

It is always easier to rest on what we have previously mastered. Sameness is certainly safe. Trying new activities, meeting new people, going to strange venues takes courage. The benefits of believing in I-Can are worth the effort. Making new friends, interacting with a younger person, experiencing a sermon from a new pastor can stimulate the mind and the heart. Both mind and heart need provocations to keep them expanding. Widows, who are adventurous, serve as role models for their daughters and for all of the next generation. Having an I-Can attitude equates to having a zest for life: by actively demonstrating that life is still worth "living", not merely enduring.

An I-Can attitude encompasses all aspects of a given situation. The stresses of any major change in life affect health. With I-Can, we, widows, can decide to...

Eat less snacks, drink less soda, prepare real meals.

Have a medical checkup, have a mammogram even after age 75.

Buy hearing aids if needed, try a free Silver Sneakers gym membership.

Get more exercise, try Line Dancing, walk around the block.

Volunteer in a church program, volunteer in a school library, volunteer in a senior center facility.

Have more fun...

Joining a hobby group, book club, Newcomer's Club, Church Circle, Travel Club

The I-Can Attitude gives permission to both a widow or a widower to honor the deceased spouse by carving out a new productive life for themselves. No spouse that truly loves unconditionally wants the one left to be miserable, grief filled for the remaining years of life. It is so much better to celebrate the opportunity to become a whole person who learns to reflect joy? Being joyful does not diminish the love for the one who has departed.

One short story about a widow-friend illustrates this message. Lucy's husband had been terminally sick for a year. He advised her to sell the house and move closer to their son when he passed. It sounded like a good plan until it materialized. Within one month, she sold her house, buried her husband, cleared out her house, and moved away from all of her supportive friends. Her son moved her into his home on the other side of the State.

Her Tunnel of Grief became a Pit of Despair with no visible avenue of escape. When I met her three months later, she was beyond miserable. She had met only a few of her son's friends, felt caged in a town where she was afraid to drive, and was certain that her son and his wife were avoiding her. When her son, desperate to help, purchased a home for her in the center of town, she was certain that he was abandoning her. She truly felt that he had cast her out of his home to a desert island.

After becoming involved in our Widows Support Group; within six months, she was reflecting a joy and independence that surprised both her and her son. She had friends again, reasons to get out of the house, other new widow friends in a new church, and a reason to live. Her conversation became what she might do to volunteer during the day.

The main point for this story is that her son appreciated that he had his mom back. He began to call her just to talk on his way to work. At least twice a week, he drove across town to run in her neighborhood. His wife invited her to babysit with their daughter. And they wanted her to join them on a week-long vacation.

Initially both Lucy and her family were doing everything they knew to do to help her. Fortunately, she rallied enough of an I-Can Attitude to come to my talk at the Senior Center by herself. Relying on the support from other widows, she met caring friends who validated her and gave her hope. Once she felt worthwhile, she was able to implement a new plan. The big message to share is that her loving husband would be proud of her metamorphosis, just as her son and daughter-in-law had become proud of her.

An Ability to Laugh at Life

The Bible calls humor medicine for the heart. From my own experiences, I understood its power. Teaching the value of humor in my own life became a powerful tool that I used when I was conversing with a new widow. After listening, I would suggest that my new friend make a list of humorous memories. "Make a journal of crazy, zany, funny occurrences. Nothing is off limits. If it was funny at the moment, put it into your notebook. These moments of laughter will become valuable pearls to tuck into your heart."

This was so apparent when I visited a long-time friend who had lost her husband two weeks before. Dean and I had lost contact with Carolyn and Don after all the kids had grown and gone. I stopped to see Carolyn as soon as I heard about Don's passing. When I mentioned the power of humor, Carolyn began to reflect on silly things that she had seen Don do in the Nursing Home during the last six months. Losing one's memory can produce strange mannerisms. As the two of us continued to reflect on Carolyn's stories, her spirits seemed to lift.

Carolyn shared with a twinkle in her eye, "I have one more story that may become the Mother Pearl." She then related an incident that happened the week before Don passed.

When she entered his room, he was lying in bed and very agitated.

"I am so glad you are here," he said anxiously.

"What's the matter?" she asked.

With his eyes furtively looking around to be sure they were alone, he whispered, I have lost my penis!"

"Oh, my! How did that happen?" Carolyn responded.

"I think those nurses took it. I can hear them talking about it on the intercom."

"Why would they do that? What do they want with it?"

"I DON'T KNOW! BUT I NEED IT, AND I WANT IT BACK!"

As Carolyn began to smile, Don emphatically responded, "Don't laugh, this is serious!"

At the end of this story, both Carolyn and I were in full belly laugh mode.

"I haven't laughed this hard in over a year," Carolyn managed to say.

"You have to put this story in your journal. It will be such a wonderful memory to get you through this next year. What a gift Don gave you before he passed...a chance to take the sting out of dementia by providing a way to laugh at the absurdity," I encouraged. "Humor is one of the best ways to heal the heart pain," I said and I hugged her on my way out.

As an addendum to this story, Carolyn and Don are made up names, but I did call and receive permission to share this story. It is the epitome of finding humor in a difficult situation.

DOOR THREE

Interpreting God's Messages Takes Faith, Not Science

Chapter 14

The Move

2015

Staying open to God's messages can be extremely unsettling, literally.

I was visiting AJ and the family in Tennessee for the Valentine's Day weekend. The family was staying in a rented condo for the year until they could move back into their Tennessee house. After the four years in Ohio, they were ready to settle permanently and chose southern warmth. The plan was to move out of the condo and back into their house when the renter's contract expired in July.

The last year had been eventful: a job change, a move in August to the Tennessee condo, a new baby in September, with another move planned in July. As frantic as it appeared, they were all doing reasonably well emotionally.

On Valentine's Day, we shared a family meal topped off with a big chocolate chip cookie/brownie for dessert. AJ and I had a chance to have a serious conversation while Caryn was putting the two older kids to bed. AJ told me that he was worried about the baby, who was now four months old. He had a neck problem that I had tried to fix at Christmas. AJ explained to me that the neck problem was only a small part of the issue. There was no grandma to visit the school for Grandparent's Day or children's choir performances at church. Ongoing, he required a grandma present in his life all the time; the whole family did. AJ wanted her to have a close relationship with all his children and share family times together. He dearly wanted family to live nearby.

We had previously had this conversation at least 50 times when he had pleaded with me to move nearer to them in Ohio, and I had said "No" as many times. He shared that they wanted to stay in Tennessee for a very long time. They certainly expected to remain in their home for at least five years.

It was a good speech, and I was impressed that he had recognized that I needed a life of my own. Although he said they were settled, I had doubts, so for the 51st time, "No," I wasn't going to move to be near them.

At that instant, I heard a very clear message in my other ear, *"You should go! It will be a good move!"* It was so loud that I turned my head completely to the left to see who might have said it. As I turned, I knew the message was from God, and it is hard to argue with God!

I immediately turned back around to AJ and said, "Okay, I am coming! I will move here." AJ was so surprised that he almost slid off of the sofa. When I explained about the message in my ear, he was a little more assured, but still very surprised since he had heard no voice...

My plans were to drive back to Ohio the next day. We all had a lively discussion in the morning before I left. Caryn and AJ were hesitant to believe that I meant it, but encouraged that I had had a miraculous change of mind! Getting a direct message from a supernatural source can be motivating if it resonates with the heart frequencies. This message did.

On the drive home, as I pondered the intensity of the message to take AJ up on his offer, I was pleasantly surprised how open I was to leaving everyone in Ohio. It seemed apparent that when I had been able to forgive and reconcile all the hurts attached to Dean's decline and passing, I had been set free. I had not realized that I had been bound to Ohio because I was holding onto fear, grief, guilt, and anger.

Chapter 15

Goodbye, Ohio

2015
February to June

I had a realtor for my house in two days and an open house the next weekend. My realtor, Theresa, was a friend of many years. I felt I had picked the best person because Theresa had sold most of the houses in my neighborhood over the past five years. She gave me a list of potential projects that might make a difference for a quick sale. I had them done by Friday. We both hoped for a deal in two weeks. That didn't happen. After two months of open houses, I agreed to lower the price.

April

    Dear God,

        I have balled up all my emotions this afternoon and squeezed them back into the cubbyholes somewhere inside my chest. They have been leaking out of my eyes all day. If I could have just finalized an offer to let me move on to the next phase, I could have held back the tidal waves. That didn't happen so I had to look at my life today and deal with the realities. Let's see…

I am walking in the footsteps of my mother. She had to move from San Jose, California by herself. She had to sell her whole world out there to be able to come here with the bare necessities. She sold her house by herself without support from any family and, indeed, no advice from any man. She was probably already sick with Leukemia at the time but chose not to mention that fact to any of us. Once in Ohio, she had to re-establish her life and make new friends, new card game partners, new neighbors, new banker, and new doctors, in a new house. Being in the same town with both her children and their families may have caused her a moment or two of angst. Would it work to fit us into her 'busy' schedule and her into ours? Most startling is that she moved here when she was 74 and died when she was 77. If I am walking in my mother's shoes, am I now in the winter of my life?

My biggest waves of emotion are not generated because I am leaving our family home, family, the church, tennis, or friends. I have been reconciling to that reality for three years, and I am okay with the logic of moving. It is the right time! Now I know the place, and it is good. I am sure that You, God, are pleased with my decision to go.

The biggest chest-pressing, breath-stopping, stomach-clenching reality is that this phase of my life is over, and I don't know what lies ahead. How did I get here? What happened to my youth? Did I make the right decisions years ago? The reality that this segment is 'in the archives,' and I can never go back was daunting today. It was one of those days, that if I allowed myself to cry, I wouldn't have been able to stop.

So, what did I do? I recognized that emotions required attention! Letting them continue to leak all over my face makes decision-making a messy ordeal. I left the house and did something that I know works very well to calm me down; I drove to McDonald's and ate a hot fudge sundae and a quarter pounder with cheese, in that order.

While it was kicking in, I drove all over the area of town where my mother had lived, even parked in front of her old house. The laughter echoed; the ethereal visions of family, who had gathered in the yard for her 75th birthday party, circled around on the front lawn.

I looked at all the smaller three-bedroom homes in that area and understood that I was following in her footsteps. But what did that mean? Logically, I realized that I am not sick; I have many things yet to do; and I have a zest for life. I will probably not be checking out in three years as she did. That was a comfort!

Coincidently, as I sat in front of Mom's house, Andrea called on my cell phone. I explained that I had been on an emotional rollercoaster all afternoon. As she had done so many times in the past ten years, she was able to encapsulate the feelings I was sharing with her. With her objective perspective, we were able to categorize the various types of emotions that were fighting for release: grief, financial worry, fear of failure, fear of forgetting important details, sorrow for leaving family and friends, and crazy self-pity that life might be worse in Tennessee than it was in Ohio. Identifying them individually, helped me to lasso them back into control. Mostly, it helped for someone to recognize that an emotional outburst could be perfectly normal. All the logic in the world may be ineffective when gigantic changes in one's life allow a typhoon of "what if's" to escape and cloud vision and purpose.

I am back to clear vision and direct purpose: get the house clean for the open house tomorrow. I got this... thanks to the trip down memory lane today and the phone call from Andrea.

Hello, my Little Dear,
   Your mother is proud of you. She knows that you will handle this move as efficiently as you do

**everything you put your mind to doing. And she
is glad you will be near family.**
Your buyer will come in due time. Stay patient.

For me to literally hear God suggest that I move to Tennessee should have produced a happy-happy/joy-joy state of mind. I should have cruised through all the moving details with no hassles and complete confidence. Wrong! I became a mess of confusion at times: what asking price, when to lower the price, who should pay the closing costs, where to live once I moved?

God got me into it, but prayer wasn't doing much to get me through it. How quickly a stressing situation could undermine all the confidence I had worked so hard to attain!

June 4

Dear Lord,

I have an offer on the house. You know what it is and whether it is good for me. I don't know yet. The people brought a contractor to estimate changes that they might want to make should the house become theirs.

It is almost anticlimactic. I was so weepy at Church on Sunday that I cried five times. It was palpable that it is the closing of an era, an end of this phase of my life. And I realized just how many good things I have done here. There was a sampling in Church of the many people I have touched with Your help, the lives I helped to change for the better.

June 5.

Dear God,

The offer was not a good offer. I would not be honoring Dean's memory by accepting that amount. It would be throwing his money away. I told them I would not counter until I had a good offer. Your comments?

I know you think I am testing you, but I am not. You are attracting the low offers by acting desperate. Don't be so locked into the idea of moving the house at any cost. Send out a message to potential buyers that this is a valuable house that deserves a relevant offer. Refusing to counter is the first step to doing that. All in good time.

Love, Your Friend

The house did sell on June 7th. The only comparison I could ascribe to my feelings of completing this major event was how I felt after I delivered my babies. Both deliveries were difficult: 23 hours for one and 14 hours for the second with contractions every 2-3 minutes. As much as I wished someone else had done that labor, the task was mine.

I could get advice on the move from others; but, in the end, all the final determinations were mine. How much of the equity had I given away to get a sale? Would I have enough after closing costs to find a house I could live in comfortably in Tennessee? It wasn't easy, but I had done it. The 'widow' had cleaned out 39 years of stuff, hired a mover, and consolidated the furnishings from an 11-room house to fit efficiently into a 6-room home. It was nearly finished.

June 20

Dear God,

This is the ending of the Ohio chapter of my life... and the beginning of what? Only You know. This is the first time in all my many years that I don't see the next 'something.'

It is interesting to be on this edge of my life, looking forward into the future filled with so many unknowns. God, I realize that all of us are standing on an edge at one time or another. We need bridges to get to the other side, to the next chapter of our lives.

'Good Bye' Note from my Dear Friend, Amy

Judy, consider these ideas when planning your move.

Take your memories; they will provide comfort and confidence.

Take the love of friends tucked away in a quiet corner of your heart.

Take the big and little victories; they provide a footpath for further successes in your new home.

Leave behind, your address, your phone number, and your assurance of hospitality for those who will come to visit.

Leave behind hurts, sadness, and any ill feelings toward anyone here.

Leave behind regrets for things not said, tasks not completed, and goals not accomplished. The negatives will not serve you well in your new home.

We love you.
Amy.

I realize I have acquired tools to use on the other side of this bridge:

- I can trust my intuitions and embrace new opportunities. That ability has served me well in the past.
- I can focus on new goals to become a better me in Tennessee.
- I can use my talents for nurturing and caregiving with others that You place in my path.
- And mostly, I can trust that You will be going to Tennessee with me. You wouldn't open this 'door' if You didn't want me to go through. If I find I need a new tool in Tennessee, I am sure You will make it available!

Lord, You know that I am a child of the 50's. Doris Day was my role model. This song has been going through my mind all day. It fits.

Que Sera Sera
Whatever will be will be
The future's not ours to see
Que Sera Sera

June 29

Moving Day

The inside of an empty house echoes like the inside of a giant cave. Maybe the echoes rebounding off the walls are really memories bouncing around free to lift off as carbonation does when the cork is popped. Must be a lot of release because they are blasting me in every room. All good mostly, 32 years in the same house…the kids were 7 and 10 when we moved here.

Dean was developing career moves…retiring…battling his monster disease…and slipping on 'home.'

I was building three very different careers…raising two kids…and learning to master widowhood. My work here is done. I feel like Dean is saying, "Time to get out of 'Dodge'. Your entourage of angels is ready to go sightseeing in Nashville!"

DOOR FOUR

Becoming Butterflies

<u>Hope for the Flowers</u> is a small allegory written in 1972 by Trina Paulus. The book is short with simplistic drawings of two caterpillars named Stripe and Yellow. It could be described as a fable for any adult wondering, "Is this all there is?" The two caterpillars learn that by accepting frightening changes prompted by love, they can leave their lives as worms to fly freely as butterflies. They can become the beautiful creation God intended for them to become...They must merely let go and let God work within them.

Of note: A Butterfly needs the individual effort it takes to emerge from her chrysalis. During the fight to emerge, she strengthens her wings, which will allow her to fly. The struggling is what yields life.

Chapter 16

No Coincidences

2017
August, Two Years After My Move

It was more than a coincidence that I landed in Haven, Tennessee in the summer of 2015. The move was good for me on many different levels. The proceeds from my Ohio home allowed me to buy rather than rent.

My new house was the first one I toured and was still waiting for me a month later. My realtor was shocked that it remained on the market; most houses were selling in one day. I wasn't surprised; it was one more verification that this is where God preferred me to be. Of course, it helped that the owner's teens had multiple containers of snakes, iguanas, and lizards in the bonus room to scare away most potential buyers. Surely, the smell of stinky clothes wafting from the boy's closets was a further deterrent. I just smiled. I was very familiar with reptiles in my home. It seemed God had orchestrated the perfect house for me to have.

Because everything was less expensive in Tennessee, all my monthly expenses (including my mortgage) were lower than they had been in Ohio. I was relieved that I would NOT need to find a job.

Haven was only one step short of Heaven. Southern hospitality became real for me. These exceptionally friendly people welcomed me into their lives, took me to lunch and invited me to parties. Active, physically fit widows were everywhere. They hiked mountain trails and rode bikes all over the Greenway. The amazing thing for me was that they saw something worthwhile in me almost immediately. People wanted to be my friend! I had lived in many different towns prior to this move and had never experienced this warm sense of belonging. Indeed, I had finally landed in Tomorrowland and found the zesty friends who had time to play.

AJ and Caryn were very surprised that within six months, I had become fully integrated into a Haven social life.

"You are so busy, Mom, you may not have time for us!"

"You just have to give me a schedule of when I can be involved, and I will be there," I replied.

The relationship with AJ and his family was one of the best surprises. It took a few months to realize that I was welcome to spend time with the grandchildren two or three times a week. Occasional sleepovers on weekends were tiring but so rewarding. To hear the kids, whisper, "Good night, Gramma; we love you," was worth all the anxiety and effort it had taken to move.

As I looked back on all the events of the last two amazing years, I realized that the springboard launching me into my current God Adventure started three weeks after moving to Haven, in July, 2015. I marshaled the courage to attend a Small Group meeting at AJ's church. A friendly lady, Arlene, stepped forward to befriend me. Arlene was an artist who had also recently moved to Haven. Both of us were trying to establish professional contacts to recreate our careers in Tennessee, Arlene with her art and me with my book and speaking opportunities. Our affinity was mutual.

The following morning, Arlene called to invite me to a luncheon with game playing. Of course, I went. The hostess, Cathy, was miserably walking on crutches after a Total Knee Replacement two weeks earlier. The fourth lady, Willie, was a demure, soft-spoken little redhead, recently widowed, who had moved to Haven to be near her son and his family.

Only a personal, interactive God could have challenged me by bringing me into contact with these three specific ladies. It could not have been a coincidence.

Meeting Cathy and witnessing how she suffered from the lack of safe effective physical therapy, opened my eyes. Inexperienced physical therapists can actually do harm in the first two weeks after surgery. I had years of experience and many highly effective ways of treating this condition than what Cathy's PT had recommended. Once I was able to decrease Cathy's pain and get her started on a productive exercise routine, I felt I needed to share my knowledge. Over the next several weeks, I wrote and published a course of powerful treatment options for knee surgery rehabilitation that could be viewed by young therapists all over the country. Indeed, God opened a potential new career opportunity with educational videos, simply by placing Cathy in my life.

Developing a friendship with Arlene was apparently God's way of easing both of us out of our entrepreneurial efforts. We seemed to realize simultaneously that selling via craft shows was not generating much profit.

During the next year, Arlene had a house built and took a job; and I launched into video development for continuing education. Arlene moved in with me until her new house was finished. The arrangement was beneficial for both of us: I offered housing, Arlene cooked and shopped to free up my time for the video projects.

Amazingly, God's biggest opportunity for me was prompted by my new friend, Willie. A few weeks after our luncheons at Cathy's had started, Willie asked if I would meet a few other widows at a restaurant. I almost said no. I was past the widowhood stresses and ready to move toward fun and relaxation in this new phase of retirement, maybe even join a new singles group.

Four of us: Willie, Mary Ellen, Marilee, and I met in a noisy, dark restaurant where conversing was difficult. As much as I did not want to revisit all the negative feelings associated with losing a spouse, I was impressed with all three ladies. They were attractive, determined to stay physically fit, and congenial. They needed a support group, but their efforts in group-building were falling flat.

When Willie and I talked the next day, I suggested that Willie's group might consider meeting in someone's home where it would be less noisy, less expensive, and more open to conversation. Willie shared that both she and Mary Ellen lived with their children and would not be able to entertain many people. Marilee still had her home, but she was not centrally located. I was very surprised to hear myself offer to have the next month's meeting at my house. I reasoned that I could get them started and then venture off to my own exciting activities, far removed from the discussions which centered on the misfortunes of being a widow.

Thirteen ladies showed up to have a delightful potluck meal the next month. Everyone had fun and said this was a good format. They would continue to come to a meeting in a home. I was pleased that I had been able to get them redirected.

"Thank you, God, for helping me entertain in my new home, but I am looking forward to our next adventure. I have met lots of friendly couples in the small group, and now these nice ladies. I am open to something quite different," I shared with God after everyone had left.

Launching into any new God adventure has generally been two vastly different dimensions for God and me. Goals inspired by God were big and required serious commitment. My choice in goals were less ambitious and only served my own needs. When Willie called a few days later and asked if I would be willing to go with her to meet the Small Group Coordinators of the church, I wasn't sure why or what to say.

Willie explained, "I want to establish our group as a small group in the church so that new widows can be directed to call me if they want to be a part of our support group. I don't speak as well as you do, and I would really appreciate your friendly presence."

I smiled and agreed to go...to help Willie. At the meeting, Willie explained herself very well allowing me to just sit back and be a presence. The two Coordinators were thoughtful but agreed that Willie and I would need to attend a Small Group Leaders Training Session. This was necessary to be sure that we understood how to be sensitive to divergent personalities and to represent the Church appropriately.

With that, I sat bolt upright in my chair, "I am just here to support Willie. I am not interested in being a small group leader for a widow's support group. I am past the support stage of widowhood!"

These ladies were good! In fact, it seemed that God had all the actors in this play well rehearsed. "Hmm, that is unfortunate. We require two leaders to work together for any small group. It provides a backup system to ensure that the group, once going strong, won't struggle if the main leader must withdraw for some reason. It also helps when a leader has someone else to confer with about activities and concerns. Of course, we are here if a serious concern needs to be addressed, but we have found that two persons are the best formula.

Would you reconsider? It sounds like this could be a very beneficial group. You would not have to meet weekly or do a Bible Study as our other small groups do. Your focus would be to help widows emerge from the grief stage to become involved in a beneficial social group."

And then all three of them looked at me and WAITED.

Chapter 17

Metamorphosis

2017
More Reflections

The Haven Widow's Group was formalized in October, 2015. Willie and I had no grand expectations to reach every widow in Haven, or to provide life-changing activities that would make this the best group anyone ever joined. We merely wanted friends who wanted to have fun and get past feeling sad.

It was a quiet start necessitated by Willie's desire to bring hurting women into a cocooned environment of respect and understanding. She, herself, needed to find meaning after her loving husband had died suddenly. She needed people to accompany her to movies, plays, and lunch several times a week. On one occasion, she shared with me, "I need to go *someplace* out of the house every day or I get too sad." Without conscious intent, Willie was living out the old adage for finding happiness: *Give to others what it is that you need yourself.*" Out of Willy's great pain, The Haven Widow's Group of 25-30 women became a fun, active, zesty group of women.

A few provisions seemed to be necessary for a widow to integrate readily. She needed to be willing to "move on", to embrace the reality that adjustments were required, and to accept that she, herself, must take the initiative. Those that chose to get involved made close friendships that allowed them to feel worthwhile and valued again.

Something magical was working. Something beyond their individual inputs was alive within this group of women. The tangibles were easy to identify and probably existed in many widow groups. They met regularly, at least once a month. Meeting for potlucks in individual homes was an incentive for the hostess to get back into entertaining for a safe group of people. The friendly atmosphere of a home allowed new people to feel comfortable quickly. In the months with inclement weather, the gathering met during the day in a conference room of a restaurant. An open structure and format of the group provided the initial unconditional love from one widow to the next.

Without Willie's heartfelt dedication to the success of the group and the desire for each new widow to find support, the group might not have been so successful. Willie kept attendance and recorded the suggestions for potential group activities. After a regular monthly meeting, she would send out an email outlining suggested places to go and things to do before the next meeting. Initially, Willie did all the planning; but before long, others began to utilize the email to ask if anyone might want to do an impromptu activity such as a movie the next Tuesday. Those interested agreed when and where to meet. The email format opened communication for like-minded people to join for specific activities that might not appeal to all in the group. The email system evolved to a dedicated Facebook page where pictures could be posted, helping everyone put names on faces. This easy communication system allowed companionship to develop that benefitted everyone.

Activities were varied. Besides potlucks once a month, they organized sightseeing excursions, plays, and senior center novelty shows. For those interested in exercise, several met for line dancing, walking a track, or weight lifting sessions. One very cold December evening, four of them took the downtown 'Art Crawl in the City' tour around the Town Square. They hurried from store to store bundled up from nose to toes to see the next display and eat cheeses. It was so cold it should have been a miserable outing, but because it was so cold, they had to laugh at their zany willingness to go, and counted it as a fun memory.

Each woman was invited to take responsibility for organizing a monthly meeting: the place, blessing, ice breaker activity, and some food preparation. Depending on the hostess's level of comfort, the meal might be in a quiet restaurant, a backyard cook-out or a sit-down dinner with fine china. Willie and I were thrilled when Angela volunteered to have a dressy New Year's Eve 'cocktail' party. Everyone brought different appetizers or gooey desserts. What a great night that was!

This format was not for every widow. For some women, the intimacy was intimidating. For personal reasons, a few couldn't assimilate and didn't stay. Some only wanted to participate in mixed groups. Some couldn't adjust to being in Tennessee and moved back to an area near long-time friends.

For those who welcomed the opportunity to develop new friendships, the support group was priceless. The monthly meeting was the backbone providing opportunities for friendships to develop around particular interests. Hobby groups splintered off and developed a life of their own. The needle point, crafty ladies were one group. Another was a book club. Several who enjoyed traveling bonded. Another group enjoyed eating lunch in different unique restaurants.

I savored the memory of one evening that illustrated the intangible benefit of creating mutual friendships. Eight of us agreed to go to Memphis to sightsee for two nights. This was the first time that these eight women had traveled together. It was also the first time that any of them had shared a room with anyone from the group. The sightseeing to all the venues went well, once we became relaxed with the idea that gathering eight women in any one place could be as challenging as herding cats.

After the second day of touring Elvis memorials and revisiting the 1960's, the group agreed to return to the motel for happy hour and snacks rather than another restaurant. We usurped the breakfast area by putting several tables together and made a feast out of food brought from our rooms. As we toasted to a successful excursion, our relaxed merriment echoed around the entire lobby. The group had been transformed from widowed acquaintances to dear friends in just two days. Retelling funny impressions brought laughter for everyone. The last man to leave the breakfast area smiled and remarked as he left his corner seat, "Y 'all have a party attitude. Enjoy your evening."

When the conversations were beginning to lag, I, serving in my role as thought-provoker, interjected a question to the group, "I am doing research. I would like you all to reflect on your own widowhood journey and share what you would tell a new widow: both the good and the bad."

At first, they were pensive. The question seemed overwhelming. Eventually, the comments came, indicating where they had been and how far they had come.

What I Would Share with a Newbie Widow

"Give yourself time to get through the grief process. Be prepared for sudden fits of tears with no warning. A beer commercial can bring on a deluge."

"Everyone will grieve differently and that is ok."

"Be aware that repressing the pain may cause physical maladies. See a grief counselor if you don't know how to release feelings."

"Pretending that everything is fine, can open a rift to depression."

"Understand that getting through the grief may depend on how long a widow has to prepare. A sudden death may create much more trauma for the wife than a long drawn out disease that allows the wife to prepare gradually."

"Even for those who have a long time to prepare, there is still that feeling of finality the moment that he passes."

"A wife who has been a caregiver for a long time should not feel guilty when she feels a sense of relief at the end."

"For some, the second year is worse than the first. It seems people become oblivious to the ongoing needs of a widow. She may feel more alone than during the first year."

"In the beginning, it may be difficult to be in the house alone at night. A security system can be reassuring."

"Wait before making any major decisions. It may seem like a good idea to move in with a daughter or son. It may seem right to give away a lot of money to the children. If she waits for a year, a widow might realize exactly what her long-term needs are."

"I gave away all my husband's tools." Linnea volunteered; "then when I bought my present house, I had to buy rakes and shovels again. I was shocked when I realized what all those tools were worth. And it would have been nice to have kept some of his big old shirts to sleep in at times."

"It never gets easier to do all the tasks that he once did, like working outside, or garage fix-up projects," Dana volunteered.

"Some tasks don't seem to get easier for me, like checking into hotels, or eating in restaurants," I commented.

"That isn't my issue," Mille responded. "I like to eat good food so I have been eating alone in restaurants all my workings years."

They were of one mind, that a widow only moves forward by choosing to adjust.

Dana: "First she needs to find new friends. I had to move to do that."

Mille: "My husband warned me that his buddies would think that I was fair game. And they did. I am so glad I moved out of Alabama."

Dana: "To get through those first few months, any widow needs to develop a thick skin. People say and do really stupid things."

Angela: "It isn't only for the first few months. My husband's older sister asked me at the last family gathering if I *missed* him! What kind of a question is that?"

Linnea: "I had trouble asking my kids for help, and then realized I would have to pay people to fix things I needed to have done."

Dana: "That brings up the whole aspect of vulnerability. Women can be taken advantage of in business dealings. I have had to buy three houses and three cars since Jake has been gone. It works better if I take a man with me, even though I do the negotiating myself."

Me: "It helps to have an identity other than being a wife. Developing a late career or volunteering can be a huge help. It is great to see Willie hosting bus trips to places like Branson for the Senior Center and for Avery to organize the wonderful day trips for us."

When there was a lull in comments, I recommended, "Ok, now share the positives of being a widow!" Without any hesitation, the comments flowed out with enthusiasm.

Widowhood Can Provide Some Great Positives

Mille: "Go with your gut. Don't just trust the advice of others. It is ok to trust your own opinions and realize your every thought does not need to go through your husband's filter."

Dana: "My husband taught me that I was allowed to think for myself about my own needs. He even told me that I was free to marry someone if that would make me have a better life."

Mille: "After all these years, I can finally make all the decisions. I don't have to ask anyone what color to paint the walls."

Linnea: "Celebrate difficult achievements. I worked with my husband in our business. It was a 24 hour-a-day marriage. When he died, I made the decision to buy a different office building for *my* business. It was scary but a good decision."

Mille: "I think it is important to get to a place where we get past the negatives, whatever they may be...maybe the last awful years of the sickness... to be able to remember the good times. Some of my friends still cling to the idea that their husband was a White Knight. That isn't healthy either."

Independence

If I could have consolidated all the positives into one word, it would be *independence*. And Willie and I agreed that over the two years of watching each of these women discard their 'Coats' of widowhood, they had become dynamic, energetic, enthusiastic individuals. Maybe the best thing about the Haven Widows was their initial hope that at some time, the grief phase would diminish to allow the expectation that each would find what her potential self could be.

As big changes were noticed in a soul-sister, the rest would join in the celebration. When Angela realized that she could choose the layout of her day, I was awestruck. She no longer had to follow the routine that she followed when her husband was in the house! And if she wanted to eat a little bowl of ice cream, she gave herself permission to do that.

The steps were baby steps, but the outcome was astounding. As I thought about my own journey without a group, I was grateful for this Haven experience. I realized that those in the group had helped me finish my own metamorphosis into a fully alive Butterfly. The dynamics of many women forging new paths… became an inspiration for everyone. All became a leader to everyone else.

My Haven ladies made me think about the story of the little boy on the beach in Loren Eiseley's (1907-1979) *The Star Thrower*, adapted by many motivational speakers. The key message is about the heartfelt actions of a little boy. A man asks the little boy why he is tediously throwing starfish back into the ocean after the tide leaves 1000's of them stranded on the beach. "You can't possibly make much of a difference," he advises.

As the little boy throws another into the surf, he replies, "It made a difference to that one."

The beauty of transforming a widow into a woman who happens to be widowed is that she, unlike the starfish, can help save the next one.

2017

Only You, God, could bring these remarkably diversified, yet vibrant individuals into this group at this particular time. That we doubted Your purpose for each of our lives in Haven, is an important factor.

All of us had hearts filled with sadness. Some suffered literal numbed functions of their bodies. Several needed medical help or psychological counseling to be sufficiently healthy to 'fly'. Length of time as a widow ranged from ten years to three weeks before becoming a cherished member. Some were able to 'fly' (including me) but none were SOARING. It took the group dynamic to encourage each one to emerge from her cocoon of widowhood into a totally new persona.

You, God, are the gardener, we are Your Marvelous Butterflies searching for the **Wonderful World of Widowhood.** We don't know the plans You have for us. In fact, most of the widows in this group don't know that I am conversing with You regularly about them.

Thank you. Me

You will see in due time...As with all I do; It will be Good. Consider that if this format has worked for the ladies in Haven, might it also work in Ohio, Pennsylvania, or California? Will love, respect, and encouragement also work for widows in other places?

The Gardener

DOOR FIVE

Learning to Love Oneself

God's Master Plan is to "Love your God with all your heart, and with all your soul, and with all your mind. This is the first and greatest commandment. And the second is like it: *"Love your neighbor as yourself."* This was eloquently explained by Jesus in Matthew 22:37-39. NIV

Chapter 18

When The Student Is Ready, The Master Will Appear

2017

Entering this new door—new chapter in my life—a gentle recap may help.

Door One: Ending my 39 years as a wife

Door Two: Emergence into the world of not-so-wonderful widowhood.

Door Three: I moved out of Ohio.

Door Four: A support group helped widows become 'Butterflies'.

Door Five: I learned to love myself just as I am.

If my story were to end here, I could have been satisfied with the new dynamics in Haven. At the age of 70, I anticipated coasting into old age. Every morning I opened my eyes to the awareness that I was still in my Tennessee house and my Tennessee world and said, "Thank you, Lord, for my good fortune!!"

But that was not the end of the story. I should not have been surprised with more mind-blowing changes in my life. That was how my adventures with God worked. He had always demonstrated a sense of humor. It was as if He whispered in my ear, ***"Don't get too comfortable in your sweet little life. I am not done with you yet. I promised you important lessons… that might turn you upside down and inside out, but that's okay. You will thank me someday."***

2017, January

After I had relaxed into my house and new life, I took a work/play vacation in Arizona the last two weeks of January. Between visits with old friends, I had five book signings/Caregiver Speaking events scattered all over Phoenix. Siri in my I-Phone became my new best friend as I navigated each different region by myself. The first day was a little scary, renting a car and driving on a busy interstate to Susie's house, but once past that first day, I enjoyed my freedom and vitality. I had booked timeshare resorts that were an easy drive to the homes of friends. I wasn't alone, but I was in control of my own time. It may not have been the best solution for all widows, but it worked for me.

I felt alive and capable in Arizona. Being in warm weather in the middle of January allowed me to recharge. It gave me uncomplicated time to exercise, enjoy nature, and think. I was able to walk at least two miles every day, in the desert, on golf paths, or on mountain trails. Talks went well with books sold. Three of my friends attended one of my talks and helped me greet attenders. What fun!

The trip was a success for fellowship, fun, freedom, and health rejuvenation. I couldn't have asked for more. But God gave me more: literally the high point of my entire life. God showed up to teach me His best lessons. These notes are what I typed into my computer my last morning before I left for the airport.

"I Met God Today"

The walk on my last day in Arizona was exhilarating. I took the path around the base of South Mountain again, but when I got to my usual turn-around point, I wasn't tired. On all the other days, I picked paths that were almost flat; but on this last beautiful Sunday, I decided to meander upward. The path came about 20-25 feet from the crest of the mountain. The slope to get to the top was quite steep and was covered with loose rocks and gravel. I had a strong urge to go to the top and felt my mind arguing with itself about the logic of doing that.

At that moment, a father and his young daughter came into view walking along the top of the crest.

"How did you get up there? Is there a path?" I asked.

The father replied, "We came up right where you are standing."

The little girl added, "You should come up. The view is very nice."

"I really would like to do that, but I didn't bring my walking stick, and I am a little bit concerned about the descent without one."

At that moment, father and daughter slipped slid sideways down the incline to where I was standing. He was carrying a splintered 2x4 that he had found somewhere along the path. His daughter had a long sturdy piece of driftwood that she was using as a walking stick.

She handed me her stick and said, "Here, take my stick. It has a really good pointy tip that sticks in the ground. I don't need it anymore. Now you can go up to the top of the mountain."

I thanked her, accepted her gift as if it were made of gold and watched them continue down the path to the bottom of the trail. I didn't hug her, but I wanted to.

As I stood at the top of that mountain with my precious stick, my mind was bursting with ideas.

First was the thought that I had just had an encounter with God. To get to the top of this mountain crest demanded divine intervention. What timing to have two people coming down at that precise moment that I was standing there. What a miracle for that little girl to give me her wonderful stick. Indeed, I felt like I had met God, and He was a 9-year-old girl with a brown ponytail wearing a pink shirt.

I sat down on an outcropping and looked over the landscape. As my little friend had said, it was a beautiful view that turned into an epiphany moment for me. Everything about my life--past, present, and future--was visible in my mind's eye as if I were looking at pictures in a book. Although specifics were veiled, my future vibrated just beyond my reach like an aurora borealis comprised of vibrant colors. I had skills, and I knew that I was meant to use them.

As I thanked God for this idyllic moment, I clearly realized that He always has my back. If I will find the faith to follow His whispers in my heart, I will continue to reach mountaintops and experience joy beyond words. Most people would have insisted that a 70-year-old woman has no business traveling by herself and certainly should not be climbing up and down mountain paths. But, what was so blatantly clear to me was that I was not alone. I was walking with God, and He wanted me to get to the mountain top where He had promised He would take me several years before.

The time I stayed there was immaterial. It may have been an hour or five minutes; I was fully in the moment. Some lasting truths became palpable.

- I was a capable female. If I could travel to Arizona and drive completely around the entire city to do caregiving talks, I was self-sufficient.

- I was unfinished. A fire for a business adventure had been lit; my age was irrelevant. If God felt I should do something big, I needed to do it. Only God knew what good I could accomplish with my efforts.

- I was not alone. As I stood up to leave, it was evident that the future world of Judy Towne Jennings was so much more than I ever dared to imagine. I realized that I was who I was meant to be on this day on the top of a mountain in beautiful Arizona. I would climb down from this mountain and embrace whatever task God asked me to do. The emotions surrounding that realization were a mixture of excitement, joy, and peaceful resolve. God is Good. He would not lead me into evil. Life, for a widow, could be Wonderful!

After Effects!

As I looked in the mirror before heading to the airport, the lady looking back at me was pretty, energetic, and eager to meet the world. This lady leaving Arizona was not the same as the lady who had arrived two weeks before. Her erect posture was strong. Her heart-light was bright.

The lady in the mirror today reminded me of a woman that I once knew 15 years ago. Today's lady looked much different from that depressed woman looking back at me while she was taking care of a very sick husband. That poor soul looked as if she herself would be requiring a caregiver soon. Her light was barely flickering.

More important than all the physical attributes, the face looking back at me today was radiant. The inner glow shining through was LOVE. Without a doubt, tapping into a source of energy from the Universe on the Mountain Top had ignited a light I didn't even know existed.

I realized I really loved the lady in the mirror. She was a good friend. And that was a concept that I needed to wrap my thoughts around and tuck into my heart for safekeeping. All really was right in my world.

I had arrived at a place in my life where I finally had sufficient love for who I was...to be able to truly love my neighbor as myself!

Chapter 19

The Power Of Free Will

2018
Reflections One Year After the Mountain Top

As I sat on the mountain, my most breath-taking Mountain Top realization was that I understood God's master plan for all His children everywhere! It was not that Jesus died on the Cross for the sins of humanity and then was Resurrected to become Lord of our lives. That was part of the PROCESS but not the GOAL.

The GOAL for God's marvelous plan is that we, His creation/His children, will choose to return to a loving relationship with God...that we will choose to love Him unconditionally with all our heart, mind, and soul.

Certainly, all of us as consummate sinners could not be allowed into Heaven. Jesus absorbed all sin present and for future generations to enable us the **opportunity** to return to God. Jesus was the example. He fully accepted all the love God had to give to him. His reaction was to love God so much that he was willing to die on the Cross for our sins. That is a lot of love!!!

God could have designed us to love him automatically, but then we would have been robots, not his children. He wants us to come to him freely of our own cognizance. He gives us free choice in all decisions throughout our lives including whether we choose to love him first and foremost.

When on the mountain, I felt like I was completely immersed in God's non-judgmental love. For the first time in my 70 years, the words of 1 Corinthians 13 in the Bible took on new meaning. I had always assumed that this passage was a directive from Christ to teach humans how to act out love for each other.

> 1 Corinthians 13:4 RSV
> *"Love is patient and kind; love is not jealous or boastful; it is not arrogant or rude. Love does not insist on its own way; it is not irritable or resentful; it does not rejoice at wrong, but rejoices in the right. Love bears all things, believes all things, hopes all things, endures all things. Love never ends."*

Not until the Mountain did I interpret this passage as an explanation of how God extends His love **first** to His own. It is this flooding of His love and acceptance upon and into us that opens our hearts and provides us with a full supply of love to pour out onto and into: ourselves...Jesus... others...and certainly, back to God!

This may not be the eschatological opinion of pastors and priests but it felt clear to me. I had an overwhelming sense of deep unconditional love on that mountain that I didn't have on my way to the top. I felt perfect at that moment in God's eyes.

It is a brilliant plan that to date, only Jesus has mastered. For God to receive love, respect, devotion, He first gives it away with no assurance of return. Only by granting us free will decisions, can we choose to return to him wholly and unconditionally.

Loving God unconditionally was, indeed, extending the same FREE WILL to God that He was endlessly extending to me. Having faith that despite any present circumstance, God's plan for me could be trusted. For me to extend unconditional love to God was my way of saying, "I will love You, no matter what!"

Trying to imagine God's Perspective, I realized that God didn't need me to grant Him Free Will. He owned it!

What He didn't own was my willingness to let Him into my world as my Friend, my Companion, my Counselor, and my Almighty Father-Abba.

And that was an 'AHA!' moment for me. His love in the form of a little girl with a stick elicited an overwhelming adoration from the core of my being for my Heavenly Father. I finally understood how this Divine Entity, the Hero of the Bible, who was able to effect mighty supernatural miracles like parting the Red Sea…could as easily touch me with soft whispers and the gift of a piece of driftwood with a pointy tip.

At that moment, as God had touched me, I wanted to touch others, especially other widows.

Pointy-tipped Stick in Arizona

Chapter 20

Love Like A Bubble Bath

2018

Of course, the challenge of any 'AHA!' moment is interjecting new truths into old relationships. Who would I be going forward in my new town? Over the next months, thank Goodness, my way of looking at my life changed.

The Major Take-Away: I recognized that I wasn't the center of my universe.

As long as I was in control of my life situation, I had very little need to check my spiritual thermometer. In fact, I was proud of how well I had been running my own life, possibly even arrogant. When all control was lost with Dean's passing, I had to admit that I needed help and turned to the "spiritual communicator within my computer". My initiation of the action to converse with God allowed me to think I was still in control.

Being on the mountain posed a Godly dilemma. When I had the encounter with the little girl and the stick, I had done nothing to instigate such a blessing. It forced me to admit that I wasn't the power-driving force in my own life. God was! He was generous and kind, but not a Heavenly Santa Claus. When I contemplated the possibility that I might need to reciprocate His kindness and love if I wanted to continue receiving His favor, it changed my motivation with church attendance and Bible study.

For the first time in my life, I read the Bible from cover to cover as part of a pastor initiative. It seemed logical that if I wanted God to be interested in my widowhood journey, maybe I should read about His biography from the beginning of time. My new realization was that I needed to treat our relationship just as special as I had my relationship with my husband. To learn God's preferences and rules might teach me to respect Him and to value His presence in my life.

The summer after returning from Arizona, I decided to be rebaptized in a full emersion pool as a statement that I was committing my life to loving Father. It was my pledge to put Him in charge.

Being honest, I did not hear whispers or see doves, or emerge to bright rainbows. By all measures, I was just a wet me coming out of that pool. Changes apparently did occur. In December, when the church offered a trip to Israel the next summer, I didn't just wish I could go someday, I signed the pledge and committed payment. In spite of the fact that I had no idea how I would accrue the funds to pay for the trip, I wasn't worried. As with all my adventures before, the finances came in from sources I hadn't expected, ahead of time, freeing me to experience the trip of a lifetime.

Our eleven-day trip was more of a pilgrimage than a vacation. There is no place better than Israel to learn about the love of God for his chosen people (Jews and Christians). I came back with a fervent love for the country, the Jewish people, and the evolving story of the Bible. What I didn't expect was that Jesus, the man, would come alive for me; he moved from my head to my heart. Following his steps from Jerusalem north, west, and back to Jerusalem filled me with inspired admiration, a sense of gratitude, and a tender respectful love for him that I never had had before. As I stood outside of a wrought iron fence surrounding the Garden of Gethsemane, my mind seemed fully aware of Jesus praying in that garden 2000 years before. A heavy sadness filled me as if I was perceiving his anguish while he prayed about his impending death the next day.

I experienced a miracle during the week, that I shared with our guide; who shared with the rest of the group. My feet were not tolerating all the walking. Mid-week, I tried to sit anytime I could because of the pain in both feet. At the Pool of Bethesda, the lesson was to leave anything bothering us there and go away with a fresh start. As I turned to leave, I realized the pain that had been nagging at me for three days was gone. In fact, I didn't have any pain in my feet for the rest of the trip. Others also experienced miracles during the eleven days.

I recognized that real love is never ending!

I extended myself to family and friends. Some responded; some did not. I had sent cards and notes to my daughter and all of the Ohio family to say that my love was never ending in spite of our distance. As an extra effort, whenever I walked past their family picture, I would whisper, "This is my beloved daughter and family, in whom I am well pleased."

Even though I was well assured of my parents' love for me as a child and also Dean's as a wife, the awareness that love escaped death was real after the mountain. The love they had toward me was unceasing and ever present!

Love is Patient and Kind.

Part of being a better child of God motivated me to make relationships right that I had harmed in my past. The first was with a young neighbor when we were both in our thirties. I had difficulty finding the woman; but when I did, the lady was happy to hear from me. The guilt for sharply worded comments was more in my head than the resentment in her mind. It turned out to be a very pleasant catch-up discussion. Kindness and forgiveness prevailed.

My second effort was to restore my relationship with a close friend who had never acknowledged Dean's passing. Again, I had difficulty locating the lady. As a last resort, I sent a letter to the friend's son with hopes that he would pass it on. He responded to let me know that his mother was not well; but had appreciated the letter. In this situation, forgiveness instilled kindness.

The third took longer to bear fruit. I had had a boyfriend, Brad, off and on for nine years through high school and college. I was the good girl, the hometown honey. He was the frat boy seeking thrills and excitement.

Ours was a strange symbiotic connection. During our college years when he was at one end of the state and I was at the other, I had several ill-omened dreams about him. When able to talk, I would ask what had happened to him the day before. He always had a calamitous report. One day, he told me his apartment had caught on fire. After a different dream, he reported that he had been in a car accident. Somehow, I always knew the bad before he had a chance to tell me.

After I graduated and took a job out of town in 1970, I expected a proposal when I came home for Christmas. He reiterated that I was the one he wanted to marry, but he wouldn't be ready to settle down for six years, not until at least age 32. I had said, "No, I NEVER want to see you again. I will find someone else. I am moving on." He had hugged me, wished me well, and walked away.

Even after I met and was married to Dean, I occasionally had a vivid dream about Brad, but only once was it excessively worrisome. I dreamed one entire night that his wife was trying to deliver their baby. Both she and the baby were struggling and in real danger. After two days of prayer and concern, I picked up the phone and called his mother. Indeed, during the dream night, his wife had been in grave danger with the birth of their baby girl. His mother was happy to report that everything worked out well.

Brad and I had had so much history that it seemed important to close that chapter of my life more amicably. Being willing to reconnect seemed to open the gate. Shortly after I tried to find him, I found a message from an unknown woman asking me to please reply. The woman was Brad's sister, requesting permission for him to contact me to offer his condolences about my husband's passing.

Updating our stories was beneficial for both of us. I needed to know how his life had progressed, and he needed to tell me. Most importantly for him was the need to tell me that although he had trouble with relationships, he was a very good father... And that his life had turned out well. He was happily settled with a good woman enjoying his retirement.

That we both had feelings of warmth and concern that continued to permeate our lives for 50 years was a heart-satisfying realization. The mutual knowledge that a person somewhere continued to believe in the other's worth felt to me like being immersed in a warm fragrant bubble bath. Realizing now that the bubble bath had been drawn by God, made me smile.

Chapter 21

Those Blessed Interconnections

The essence of my widowhood journey is that it brought me to the most important awareness of my life to date. I had arrived at a place where I could joyfully say that I **could accept whatever path I found myself walking.** That was the *big love story* I thought God wanted me to live and share. That is the story that Christians hear in every church sermon, but have great difficulty internalizing it, personally. It is easy to be grateful for the blessings in one's life: sweet puppies, new babies, reconnections with old friends. Accepting that the death of a spouse, murder of a child, deteriorating illness, or even a leaky toilet can be a part of God's plan stresses faith to the limit.

I saw this unfold on an autumn photo shoot with Caryn, AJ, and the kids. Given that the three children were overly 'sugarized' due to Halloween, I only saw erratic, goofy misbehaving. The possibility that any picture on that day would show the true worth of my grandkids seemed highly unlikely. We would be lucky if we didn't lose one of them in the creek.

Days later viewing the proofs, I realized that a true artist sees beyond the surface to the perfect spirit within, as does God. The blessed energy, individualism, and simple naiveté of each of my grandchildren burst out of the pictures. What a wonderful family I had. If Halloween sugar can be turned into a moment of family unity, what greater good could God do with truly broken lives?

Photographer: Kristin Amaro, **afH Capture+Design**

Picture of Judy's Family

The crystal-clear spiritual message in this picture completely filled up my heart with a perfect love. As Caryn said when she sent the family picture, "This picture is such a window of you at this time of your life." And it was. I realized that this family was my charge. It was my task to love them unconditionally, sugar and all. If I could do that well; they, in turn, might believe that God has continually loved them just as they are. My greatest wish was that all my grandchildren would know my God personally, interactively, to the extent that they would recognize whenever He would send them a miracle. At some time in their lives, I hoped they would have Mountain Top adventures of their own.

Grandparenting can be an exquisite partnership. Where else can such a magical connection be forged? Reciprocal love is never guaranteed; it takes work, but worth the effort. For me, the connection felt Heavenly designed.

It was only recently that I was able to live near my son's family. In Ohio, I had been a big part of my other grand-girls' lives. Leaving them behind had been difficult. As I thought about our close relationship, I was certain that it was not an accident that each of them was a part of my family...and I was their grandmother.

One very powerful memory catapulted to the front of my mind as I contemplated the many unexplainable situations with my grandchildren that had occurred over 12 years. The most profound interaction happened the summer before Dean passed, when Cindy was five.

Dean had been too weak and feeble to do any fun activities that summer after the flood. In early July, I asked him if there was anything on his Bucket List that he wished he could have done. Without hesitation, he answered, "The Football Hall of Fame! Do you think we could drive and spend a day there, and then drive to the family camp where the family will be? We haven't been to camp for several years, and I would like to see all of our old friends."

I made some calls to see which day would be best for our daughter and her family.

Sarah suggested Friday because both she and our son-in-law had other duties and would appreciate help watching the girls in the afternoon. It was arranged. The sightseeing at the Football Hall of Fame on Thursday had proven wonderful but exhausting. The next morning, Dean slept in the car from Canton to the camp, ate a congenial lunch visiting with old friends, and then napped in a lawn chair on the beach.

With Dean settled, I had undivided time to play with the girls in the swimming area quadrated off with peers. It was a large beach-pool area with a varied depth of water from 2 inches at the beach to 5 feet by the dock. At the ages of five and six, both girls had passed the lifesaver's swim test the first day of camp, meaning that they had full swimming privileges. Unfortunately, passing a 2-minute test might have provided a false sense of security for the youngest, Cindy.

That particular year, another family with older children had brought a huge circular floaty that could hold at least nine children. Cindy, by far the youngest, would not stay away from the bigger kids in the float.

After watching the rough play of the older children, my heart was telling me that Cindy was in danger. When the "King of the Raft" shenanigans started, I hurried out onto the dock next to the raft and watched. Sure enough, Cindy was dumped out and came up under the raft. When she came to the surface, her head was being held under the water. She could see above the water but did not have the wisdom to figure out how to go back under and swim away from the raft. Her eyes latched onto mine with a look of abject terror.

In two seconds, I was in the water, grabbed Cindy and pulled her out of the water. Knowing that I had to leave camp that afternoon, and Cindy might be tempted to play in or near that raft again, I looked directly into Cindy's eyes and said, "You get up on that safe beach! Don't you EVER go near that raft again! The next time, I won't be here to save you!"

So many times, over the years, I have thought about that day:

What if...my very sick husband hadn't begged to go see the football museum?

No other request would have been worth honoring.

What if...we had not selected THAT day to visit the family camp that week?

What if... I had not trusted the ugly feeling that I had in my heart urging me to watch Cindy every second? No lifeguards could have seen her from the angle where she came up, and none of the nine children would have missed her.

Cindy very possibly would have drowned.

Fortunately, on that day, the God-made heart-connection worked. I was designed to be Cindy's grandmother at that camp to save my granddaughter's life. No other explanation could explain the course of events leading to that final result. I reasoned that God must love Cindy very much and have great plans for her life. What an honor to be selected as a tool in that God-moment that day.

It was a satisfying awareness to realize God had placed me into the lives of my other grandchildren for specific reasons as well. Some were already realized: two of the seven were born with severe wry neck problems that I was able to resolve. I was grateful that I was in Ohio to help for the first two years with the two adopted boys. I had a chance to bond with them before my move.

How many other blessed interconnections, listed in God's To-Do Book, were yet to surface like Cindy in the water? What a scary thrill that I could be God's instrument to shape their lives. Scary! Because I was afraid I might discount any heart urgings if I was not purposely tuned in.

When I moved to Haven, I had hoped for a pleasant relationship with AJ and his family. As relationships with all three kids are developing, I realized that 'pleasant' was the wrong goal. Over the coming years, I might need to be the one to rescue one of them from a bad situation, look him or her directly in the eyes, and say, "You get up on that safe 'beach'! Don't you EVER go near that (blank) again! The next time I might not be here to save you!"

That awareness allowed me to see very clearly what a noble role it was to be a grandparent...a chance to love grandchildren as a partner with God.

DOOR SIX

Adventures With God

God's Master Plan is to *"Love the Lord your God with all your heart, and with all your soul, and with all your might."* Deuteronomy 6:5 RSV

Chapter 22

Being Real

December 2017

Over the two years of committing formally to helping Willy develop the Widow's Group and informally developing close friendships with several diverse women, I found that I had become immersed in a heavy group-think. Constantly presenting the wonderful side of widowhood with an upbeat persona became my norm. It wasn't that I didn't recognize how blessed I was to be in Tennessee with my dynamic friends; I did. It was, more so, that I was wearing my "happy widow" demeanor as a mantle. It had become my new 'Coat' of Widowhood.

Toward the end of the year when I turned to writing for hours-a-day, I should have recognized that something was out of sync. Initially, I had immersed myself in writing about the potentially wonderful world of widowhood as reflected in the transformations in the lives of my friends. I truly believed I could transpose all the exciting adventures over the past two years into an inspiring story that would surely give all other widows hope. After all, wasn't Haven Utopia? Weren't we all happy and satisfied Butterflies?

Oh My, how naiveté and denial abound!

By the end of 2017 I felt as if I was either a fraud or mentally unbalanced. I was ready to give up my project! The task had become an agonizing ordeal! I realized that to mentor anyone into true happiness, required that the person had to choose to transport herself through that door. I was NOT giving my friends the same free will that I had found for myself on the Mountain. I was playing at being God. The formula to pour out an immense amount of unconditional acceptance onto another person without expecting anything in return had fallen away. The wellbeing of my friends had become my mission. I took charge. Would I never learn to "Let Go and Let God!"?

Oh, Dear Lord, why are Your tasks for me so heart-wrenchingly difficult? A simple story about the success of our widow's group has been a year-long roller coaster. Angela hugged me yesterday and told me that I am her hero! She thinks I am the merriest widow that she knows. Little does she know that I still experience sadness. I have become a happiness clown playacting for those around me, hoping to take their sadness away.

Why couldn't I stay on the mountain with You forever? You have urged me to empty out my heart and mind completely, to start over with everything I thought I knew.

The excruciating problem is the peeling off of the layers of my heart and mind to get to the kernels of truth deeply buried in my soul. At times, I have felt like I was doing an appendectomy on myself and the damaged tissue was well rooted to the good parts.

Can any human ever become REAL and authentic? Is it possible on this side of Heaven to have the outside smile reflect an inner joy...not a painted-on mask?? I would like to stop doubting who I am, what I believe about You guiding my life, and what I need to do to be Your cherished child for all the rest of my days on earth!

Who am I to think I could share Your insights, Lord? UUURG!

Oh, Child. Why do you doubt so quickly? I promised I would help you with every word if you would let Me. Am I expected to condone anything other than the ultimate truth about My character, Christ's love, and your task? I am not sorry for the difficulty of this task. All the searching was necessary to bring you to a righteous conclusion, a wisdom worth sharing.

You are not done with the rough road. It might help if you itemized your boulders along the way...share your feelings! It is the only way that you will truly have a clear vision of what you have achieved. And you will need clear vision to take the big steps forward because your story is all widows' story: victorious moments are frequently followed with fits of wallowing in the pits of despair.

All my children bounce from high moments to doldrums. You are unique because your highs can go higher and your lows much lower than most. Sometimes within a day or an hour. I am smiling, My little lamb. That is one of your characteristics that makes you special to Me. You can provide a realistic example for others to observe.

Who you are is paramount to your task. You wrote about the 'Doors' or stages of one's life. They represent life changes and choices. Trust your walk. It is ok that it is personal to you. Mandatory, in fact. It gives others permission to accept their own walk.

Never the less, you have reached your Haven, a peace with Me. Don't minimize how far you have come. Certainly, we have many more 'Adventures' yet ahead. Embrace all of them. The Joy within the Journey is what is most important. You have done that; don't be afraid to be another person's hero. That is your gift to them. You are My front-runner. Be willing to share the difficulties that are inherent with change. Being REAL will help those who are watching you. If you are anxious and apathetic, consider the possibility that some of your friends are as well.

And always remember that I won't force any of My children to go through any of their 'Doors'. That is their Free Will. All I can do is guarantee that if they let Me, they will not go into the next stages of their lives alone.

"Oh, Lord! Is this worth it?!"

If you sincerely want Me to answer that question, you must first answer My questions.

Do you love Me?

Did you enjoy your Mountain Top adventure?

Do you think that your personal God can love all people as you feel you are loved: interactively?

CAN YOU SEE WHERE THIS IS GOING?

Do you think others would be willing to have adventures, as you call them, with their version of Me, if they knew how to do that?!

OK THEN...

Do you care for others who may need Me: your family, your widow friends, even people who are looking for Me in Timbuktu?

Can you think of a way that you can share what you have learned these past few years without making this story public...even if you get criticized by some people?

Your Cherished Friend

So, the attempt to be real commenced.

Chapter 23

Let's Do This

2017-2018

You had me with *"**Do you love Me?**"*, Lord. I can't **Not** do this. Just one more question as I finish my writing: Pastor's sermons are always messages about the centrality of Christ in our lives...but I don't picture Christ in my mind when I converse with You. Is that wrong?

You were not commissioned to write about the entire eschatology of the Trinity. Not in your wheelbase. Above your pay grade. Your central message is Christ's answer to the Disciples' question: "Which is the greatest commandment?" His answer to them and to you is "Love the Lord your God with all your heart, and with all your soul, and with all your might." Deuteronomy 6:5 RSV If Jesus, Himself, told you to do this, can your loving book about Your cherished God be wrong? Jesus knows your heart.
Can you finish Our task now?

Yes, I think I can.

So, what happens next?

Your little One

Two events in one week, seemed to cement the wisdom in my heart to let me know that I had, indeed, developed the clear vision that God had intended for me to achieve. The first part of the first event was listening to the author, Eric Metaxas, speak about his book, ***Martin Luther.*** Mr. Metaxas shared Martin Luther's premises on sin and a relationship with God. No human can become sin-free as Martin Luther realized when he almost lost his mind trying. A person doesn't have to become perfect to have a relationship with God. Jesus bridges the gap, and nothing anyone can do improves on that fact. The second part of this event: I read and consumed the 600-page book about Luther. It was energizing for me to realize that a learned scholar like Martin Luther had to trust that God had a plan for his life no matter how far from his expectations that path had led.

I wanted to grab the hands of my friends and tell them,

"God loves you. Everything you can possibly think of will work out all right!

Whether the situation is caregiving for someone with dementia to finding a second perfect husband...

Whether struggling to pay all the monthly bills to buying a sweet little red car...

Whether trying to patch up the holes in the heart from an abusive marriage to finding a sweet puppy who idolizes you...

Everything is there inside each of us to verify God's perfect plan...

Secondly, I watched a movie about love in action: **Same Kind of Different as Me** based on a novel with same name by Ron Hall. The wife of a wealthy art dealer (Ron Hall) restores her marriage and many other lives by demonstrating the love of Jesus to the homeless in her community. She didn't berate her husband and cast him out because he had had an affair. She didn't rebuke the felons in the mission and tell them that they were going to Hell if they didn't change their ways. The wife became their friend as God had done with me: non-judgmentally. The powerful message was that because the wife loved first, just as God loves first, people changed...of their own free will, not because God commanded it.

'Seeing' who I was to the God of the Universe made me realize that after being upside down and inside out, I had purged all the negatives associated, not only with losing my husband and my identity, but layers of misinformation and hurts from my past. It was freeing.

Taking Action

My own choices first. What could I do to demonstrate that I had chosen to have an adventure with God?

Gratitude

I could show gratitude for tangible evidence that indicated to me that God was actively working in my life. I could take pictures of beautiful rainbows and sunsets and post them on my Facebook page. I began to collect coins that I found on the ground and reported to friends when I had found one. The "In God We Trust" was evidence for me on each coin.

On one walk, I found a penny next to a truck by a mailbox. As I bent to pick up the penny, I noticed that a seasoned, gray-haired man was standing in the yard. Although I had never met the man, I walked to him and gave him the penny. He was a bit startled at my gesture. "I found that penny next to your truck and thought it might be yours. Did you notice what it says on that coin?" I asked.

He looked at the penny and read, "In God We Trust."

"Yup!" I responded with a smile on my face and walked away. His face lit up in understanding and he also smiled.

Fine Tuning Myself

Early mornings became a treasured time to place earphones on my head and walk for two miles. I had forgotten how good the walks were in Arizona. Over a 10-week time, I learned how to dress for 43 degrees to 75 degrees. People along the route were greeted whether I knew them or not. It was a time with God to pray and listen. I shared with my widow friends how much better my joints felt because of the walking exercise. Some had already started to walk daily and agreed.

Sharing My Adventure with God in a Book

The task I felt I was given when I came back from the Mountain was to write a book for widows. I felt the charge was to boldly describe amazing 'miracles' that I had personally experienced over my past years as a widow. The process of writing the book was the conduit to allow me to speak to various widows in different settings. In a small Methodist church, three of us partnered with the pastor to welcome widows in the church and community to come to a breakfast talk. After sharing with the group that I felt I had literally heard the Lord speak to me about moving, one lady in the audience asked the pastor if he had ever "heard" God speak to him? His response was, "Yes, I have experienced two audibles." It was an eye opener for everyone.

My writing duty was to make the 'Adventure with God' phenomenon readily believable. Surely if I could experience 'miracles', ANYONE could. If others realized God was real and He acted regularly in THEIR lives, the door to a love relationship with God might open for many more people. And wouldn't that make God happy? Maybe others would share their stories and throngs of widows might start finding pennies along their paths. Those thoughts made the hair on my arms tingle!

Chapter 24

Frank

Dear God,

If I could, I would draw an outstanding word picture that totally, inexplicable leaves NO doubt that You work adventures for us. Events are set into motion without our knowledge that create an almost magical feeling. Sometimes the event is so ludicrous it makes no sense. Sometimes, it pushes us to take on a task that seems beyond our capabilities, far from our comfort zone.

For me, I wouldn't have taken on many projects without Your promptings. When barriers have sprung up that seemed insurmountable, an amazing remedy has always surfaced. And to the credit of the adventure, I am always better for participating.

Can you suggest such an example?

I

I gave you a perfect example last September: Frank.

I should not have been surprised that sharing about Frank was a perfect example of a God-Adventure. First, in my experience, God had a very good sense of humor, enjoyed the unexpected, and on occasion used outlandish unconventional events to open the heart. That was certainly the case with Frank. Any normal pet, such as a puppy or kitten is easy to love. In contrast, it takes a tremendously expansive amount of heart to fall in love with a pig.

Frank

Late in September I joined the family to celebrate little AD's third birthday. On the way to the restaurant, AJ stopped the car in a shopping center parking lot to let the kids see a bevy of baby pigs that a local pig raiser was selling out of cages. Emi wanted to hold one and picked out a little black runt. She and the runt snuggled immediately together into a chair. Seeing that look on Emi's face, I knew we were all in trouble. Who doesn't love baby animals?

When AJ suggested that I might need a little pig at my house, I emphatically said no pets of any kind were welcome. Caryn and I both encouraged AJ to end the visit and continue on to the restaurant. She and I were obviously not tuned to the God Frequency that AJ and Emi were. "Mom, just hold this little guy; he is really striped differently." AJ insisted. I sat down and the pig man put the 12-week old male, chipmunk striped, micro pot belly pig in my lap.

Little did I know that holding Frank would melt my heart. He was snouty, bristly with course spikey hair, awkward, and skittish any time his feet were off the ground. In my lap; however, he was a cuddly little ball of pleasure. And my heart opened effortlessly, instantly.

Two were chosen, why not three. Anyone making the decision to buy a pig as a pet must either be looney-tunes or inspired by a Supreme Source. In hindsight, it must have been a special whisper to AJ, because Caryn and I could not dissuade him from buying three little pigs.

The next morning, I wrote on Facebook:

> "The heart is a very strange organ. It can grow with exercise. It can grow with love. I have a new love. His name is Frank. He snorts when he sleeps. He loves milk and crackers. And he is not sure that he loves me yet. No, Frank is not a handsome boyfriend. Frank is a micro pot belly pig.
>
> This has opened up new challenges in my life I never expected. For some reason, my son determined that his family had to have three little piggys, and I have pig duty tomorrow for the morning feeding. The Lord works in very strange ways. I am not recommending that all widows fall in love with a pig. I can recommend finding something that stirs the heart, and it might be easier to kiss a pig than a 'frog'."

I

Ok, why is 'Frank' an adventure?

This little story is an unconventional statement that love works. The kids had an instant overzealous love for their pets. They rocked them like little babies, snuggled with them during TV breaks, and played chase in the back yard. All three children learned that baby animals need gentle care and attention. They learned that modifying a piggy's free will choice to run is far easier with Cheerios treats, than trying to catch a pig from behind. Overall, at this point in time, three little pigs were a God-send for three lonely kids in a new house.

These pigs, in spite of their messiness and expenses, became a project to get all family members united for one purpose: integrate outdoor critters into a family. AJ had care duties, Caryn shopped for sweaters to keep them warm during outdoor play times, and Grandma trained them to respond to treats (Treat-training to go up and down steps and, more importantly, to come when called.)

Least expected and something only God could know was that the three little pigs loved to cuddle and kiss to show affection. When really happy, they wagged their tails and smiled. Everyone who encountered them was touched.

Happy Piggys

Chapter 25

Three Cinderellas And One Prince

2018
January

Although all the widows in the group had had positive life changes, I had to ask, "What happens next for them?" Could they be acting on God whisperings? If so, did they recognize the source of those urgings?

Mille bought a lake house and spent many hours with her extended family making it livable. It was proving a positive choice for everyone involved.

Willie volunteered to host trips sponsored by the Senior Citizens Center. She became the shining light on the hill for those meekly willing to try travel excursions.

Avery took in her niece and grandnephew, Baby Drake, during their post-divorce adjustment. They were thriving on her loving kindness.

BUT! Did God have any 'Franks' placed shrewdly along their paths that could melt their hearts and eventually take their breaths away? For all of them, was love from another man in their future? What if there was a huge 'door' labeled *Falling in Love*? Would any have the courage to venture into a dating relationship? Would the support group be willing to support them in such an intense endeavor?

Several women from the past two years flashed into my head. I pictured them as mature Cinderella's.

Violet

I moved into my new house in July. Over the next few weeks, I took excursions around town to locate new grocery stores, hair salons, and other needed businesses. Neighbors suggested that I check out the Labor Day weekend festivities on the Downtown Square. My intent was to sample the festival in case I decided to take friends with me the next year.

Exploring the food kiosks and small band area only took a few minutes. On my way back to the car, I meandered to the pavilion and sat down on a bench to listen to the music before leaving. Within a few minutes, a nicely dressed elderly lady sat down next to me on the bench. She introduced herself as Violet and the man sitting next to her in a lawn chair as her husband, Bob.

Why the conversation swerved to their love story, I couldn't fathom. It was not usual to find myself involved in an in-depth personal story within five minutes of meeting a person. Maybe Violet was feeling sentimental that day. Maybe I looked lonely and in need of a friend. Maybe God was delivering a message I would need to consider at a later time.

Violet told me that she had only lived in Haven for four years. Bob was her second husband; although, she had dated him many years back at a small college in Indiana. They had been very much in love at that time and wanted to build a life together, but her mother forbade it. She ended up marrying another man and having children. Bob had also married and moved away from Indiana.

After her husband died, Violet went back to her college Homecoming event with friends and un-expectantly reconnected with Bob. He introduced her to his wife as his college girlfriend. It surprised her to realize that she had flutters in her heart when he smiled tenderly at her as he described their relationship during their youth.

Bob called occasionally over the next two years, to "just stay in touch"; then, she stopped hearing from him. Six years to the day that they had reconnected for Homecoming, she answered the doorbell to see Bob standing at her door. When he came in, he explained that his wife had died, and he was certain that he didn't want to live one more day without her in his life. He had never stopped loving her and hoped that she would become his wife for the time they had remaining. She married him two weeks later and moved to Tennessee.

I asked if she would be willing to tell me how old she was when that happened. Violet smiled and said, "I was 75 and he was 77. We both have some health challenges, but it has all been worth it!"

Daisy

Daisy was a gregarious, considerate, attractive woman in her sixties. She shared with me that she had been widowed for 5 years and wondered if I ever considered finding someone with an online dating service. Daisy wanted to date but was very afraid to venture into the dating world. She had heard horror stories about lying, cheating men that are not who they say they are. Her best friend had remarried only to find out that her new 'wonderful' husband made his living by marrying wealthy women and then divorcing them in about five years for a nice settlement.

One evening Daisy and I took a dating lesson from my friend Dana. Dana showed us the sites that were most likely used by men who were seeking long-term commitments rather than casual sex. Dana explained what a guy might be really saying in his profile (from her experience). Someone with no interest in exercise, looking for a partner who was a good cook, might mean he tended to be overweight, possibly in less than adequate health, and really wanting someone to care for him in his failing years. That might not be a negative, but it shouldn't be a surprise.

As the three of them talked and reviewed profiles on Dana's tablet, the conversation seemed to drift into all the negatives with few of the positives encountered with online dating. At the end of the evening, Daisy hugged me, thanked me for the informative evening, and said she would have to give serious thought to trusting her heart to a profile in a computer program. It sounded too dangerous to venture into that arena without a security team to help her make solid decisions.

Rose

Rose attended the Widow's Support group in November, two months after becoming a widow for the second time. She was a soft-spoken beautiful lady in her early 80's. In her introduction to the group, she explained her present circumstances so wonderfully that everyone who was present wanted to hear the rest of the story.

"I had been married to my first husband for 50 marvelous years before he passed. We were both 72. I never expected to find love again, but I did. I fell madly in love with the man who became my second husband. We shared three wonderful years together before he recently passed.

When people tell you that love can be as exhilarating in the senior years as in youth, they are telling the truth. I am now eighty and wonder if I might yet fall in love again because there is no expiration date on the need for passionate love."

When I could meet with Rose privately, she was very willing to share her story in more detail. She had had a good marriage with her first husband, Joe, until he developed dementia. For the last ten years of their marriage, he was 'absent', leaving Rose very much alone in their marriage. When he passed, their daughter insisted that Rose should search for a new partner and helped her submit a profile to *Love.net*. (fictional company)

"Without my daughter's help and encouragement, I wouldn't have had the courage to date. I had to decide if my need to love and be loved died with my husband. When I realized that it had not, I stuck my toe into the pool of internet dating services. *Love.net* seemed to have more men interested in commitment than those only looking for one-night-stands."

I asked, "How did you let the men on the site know that you were not interested in those that only wanted the one-night-stand relationship?"

Rose smiled and explained, "My opening comments on my profile read 'A 72-year-old practicing Catholic lady. This picture tells you that what you see is what you get.' I didn't use an old picture or a glamour shot. The picture was a selfie taken the day that I submitted my profile. It worked."

She continued, "The profile asked for preferred distance; I left it blank. I reasoned that if any gentleman were sufficiently interested, he would be willing to make the effort."

I asked, "What happened after you submitted your profile?" With a twinkle in her eye, I said, "The world of adventure began. I met many charming men. Several from Knoxville drove to meet me. One was an author and very interesting. Another came from Mississippi, two from Alabama, and several from Fairfield Glade. I was seeing two others who were very nice men when I met BOB. I knew I liked him at our first meet at a coffee shop. There was more chemistry with him than anyone else I had met. He was quite attractive from my perspective and seemed to be interested in me.

I wanted to know how she knew she could be happy with him. Rose answered that it is always a gamble. "Bob was polite, shared my interests and lifestyle choices at this stage of our lives, and made me feel as thrilled to see him as I had been when I fell in love with Joe.

I commented, "It is so sad for you to lose another loving man. I don't know that I could go through the loss again?"

Rose replied, "I feel we all are to live each moment of our lives to the fullest as long as we are here. You are correct. Had I not married Bob, I wouldn't have become a widow for the second time. But, I also wouldn't have had the three years of wonderful memories. I think our being together kept us vital. His passing was proof of that. The brain scans after he was admitted to the hospital for a fall on a Sunday morning, revealed that his entire brain was riddled with tumors. He never recovered after the biopsy the next Wednesday. The doctors didn't know how he could have functioned so normally for those three years. I like to think my love energized him. I know I was motivated by his desire for me."

She continued, "Nothing can compare to the ecstasy of sharing a passionate love. What is sad is that too many widows are afraid to expose themselves to the possibility of falling in love. They have been brainwashed to believe that they do not deserve to be in love after they become widowed. And that is just not true! In fact, the incredible reality of widowhood is that a woman is set free to fall madly in love with another man.

I don't know what my purpose is at this stage. Maybe I should mentor other widows and give them the encouragement that my daughter gave to me. I genuinely believe that a perfect man is waiting in the wings for any widow who wants to marry again."

WAYNE

Understanding my friend, Wayne's, situation was heartbreaking. Dean and I had been friends with Wayne and his wife Carolyn for many years. When Dean became ill, I elected to use Wayne's financial planning advice to allow me to stay home with Dean sooner than I had planned. His personal guarantee that I would be financially secure was reassuring. And, indeed, over the years, his advice had proven excellent.

On a visit to Ohio the previous year, I was dismayed to learn that Carolyn had passed suddenly. Wayne openly shared that he was completely lost and did not know how to survive the overwhelming sense of loss he was feeling. I listened and shared as tenderly as I could about my own journey. When I left him, I hoped he would find mentors and support help from some sources near him.

The next year, on my annual visit back to Ohio for a financial checkup, I found him in much better spirits. Wayne shared that for several months during the last year, he was nearly worthless. He stayed at his office late into the evening to avoid going home. Unfortunately, being at the office didn't help. When a Hospice counselor called to invite him to a support group for twelve Tuesday evenings, he went. Each session seemed to bring him out of his pit a few degrees. By the end of the twelve weeks, he understood his grief and what he could do to get beyond it. He actually had regained sufficient motivation to take the trip to Israel that he and Carolyn had planned to do together before she became ill.

While on the tour, he felt so sad that he merely moved from the bus to a scenic area and back to the bus, until...he entered one of the churches built to commemorate a miracle that Jesus had done there 2000 years before.

Something happened. While sitting in that church, Wayne felt something change in his body. He began to sweat. He became light-headed. His mind became so focused on what was happening to him that he had to be roused to attention to get back onto the bus. When he got up to leave, the heaviness and despair in his heart was literally all gone. He told me that he had no other explanation than a miracle. I was thrilled to hear that his grief was released.

"No, that is not the whole story!" Wayne continued. "I met someone later on that trip that I have developed feelings for. She has come to visit, and even met my family."

"Oh, my goodness!" I exclaimed. "I am so excited for you. I believe so strongly that the second-time love can be as powerful as the first young love. Good for you. I have chills all over my arms!" I said as I rubbed both of my arms to calm the chills.

Wayne added, "I am so surprised with my openness with you and your excitement. You don't understand that you are the only one that seems to think this is a big deal for me."

I smiled. "I understand! You still need to be cautious as anyone should be. Talk to your attorney before you make any big decisions. She should as well. I truly do think passionate love can heal the heart and soul."

Wayne queried, "If you feel that strongly, why are you not dating? You are still young. What are you waiting for?"

I responded that I had found a second love and shared my story with Wayne. When I spoke at the library in my home town in 2017, a man tapped me on the shoulder and said, "Remember me?" I recognized him immediately even though I hadn't seen him in 40 years. He had been a childhood friend that I later dated when I was in graduate school. We should have married then, but careers got in the way. Fear of such a powerful relationship when we were so young scared both of us, and we parted sharply.

He had read in his paper that I would be speaking and chanced reconnecting. We had a three-hour lunch to catch up. I felt like I could have talked to him for three days. Reconnecting with him felt like reconnecting with the other half of my own soul. He felt the same. For two months after I got home, we talked for hours on the phone. I became as giddy as a teenager waiting for his calls. Hopes for a full life with him began to creep into my heart.

Unfortunately, our timing was off again. He had a farm, another business, and little grandchildren that depended on him. I had my life in Tennessee with my family and commitments. When it became apparent that any relationship would be a forever friendship or nothing, we selected the friendship.

That door to a committed relationship closed again, but if it reopened in the future, I would very possibly step through to explore whether we still had any possibility of a life together. He was the last man that I would let into my heart. I was not interested in dating anyone else.

Chapter 26

A Haven For Butterflies

"I can do all things through Christ who strengthens me."
Philippians 4:13 NKJV

2018

I woke up with a BIG thought one morning as if God had tapped me on the back of the head. What if the whole purpose of our Haven Widows Support Group was to learn how to support every woman on her journey even if that journey made her a WIFE again. The thought was so far removed from how I knew widow's groups generally operated that it had to be divinely inspired.

Partly determined by Rose's strong endorsement for a second love and partly from provocative questions that I had posed to the group at various get-togethers, I realized needs were being ignored.

One of Angela's comments got my attention. "Sometimes, I find myself wondering if I will ever be kissed passionately again?" During the next month's group discussion time, I queried the group, "Do you feel widows and widowers are allowed to fall in love again late in life?" After a few long seconds of quiet, the room erupted into a lively discussion. One conversation thread was what to do if a man or woman 'hits' on one of them. Some of the stories that people were willing to share brought smiles. Old ladies being approached by awkward gents can be better than Candid Camera skits. After the laughter abated, a very new widow wiped her eyes and said that she had not laughed that hard in three years.

It was apparent from the zesty comments that several of the women were curious about dating. Their discussion served as an icebreaker on the subject, not a proclamation that marrying again was required for happiness. For this group at this time, sharing about deep concerns was valuable.

On a later evening, I forged ahead with a different question. "Have you all given yourselves *permission* to love again?" The room went deathly quiet. A few confessed that they had wondered if they would find love again, or if they would be alone for the rest of their lives. Some shared that they would never be able to tolerate being touched by another man; their husbands had been their soul mates. No men could take their places.

Some in the group had dated. Dana admitted that she had and shared some of the details of what that was like for her. Two women volunteered that their husbands had asked them to promise never to remarry. One other woman mentioned that her adult son had pooh-poohed any consideration of her finding another mate. For his mother to contemplate dating with the purpose of remarrying was entirely unacceptable to him! This awareness of her son's aggressive disdain forced her to see gentlemen in secret. Until this discussion, she had felt uncomfortable disclosing the fact that she chose to date and even considered finding another love. "I was worried that if people knew I was dating, I would be asked to leave," she admitted. Indeed, some other widow's support circles made it a policy that members who started to date would need to remove themselves from the group while actively dating.

The majority of the women felt that widows should not feel guilty if they yearned to find companionship with another man. They also felt that adult children had no right to disparage a parent from seeking love. One of the women shared that when her mother became a widow at the age of 64, the mother's friends and siblings told her that she was a strong woman and certainly did not need a man in her life. At the age of 85, she insisted on marrying a man she professed to love. Unfortunately, it was the wrong man at the wrong time in her life, and the marriage caused many problems for this lady. "Now, I wish we all would have helped Mom find a new partner when she was younger. We had no idea how unhappy she was after my dad passed." Most adult children don't truly understand the loneliness a widow endures.

The Butterfly Garden

Rose made a profound impression on me. She looked and carried herself as if aged 60 instead of 80. Confident of her worth with no problem entering into a conversation with strangers, Rose felt all widows deserved to find a new loving mate. She was a true inspiration for this group of widows!

I was not surprised that Rose had come into the group at the perfect time to be a role model for re-finding love. That deserved a big thank you to God. If Rose and I could help one or two women become positive examples by stepping out in faith, everyone might benefit. More importantly, the adventure to find companionship could occur within a supportive group of friends.

My big earth-shaking, super, God-inspired directive was to purposefully attempt to support women who wanted to date, within the security of the support group. Over a breakfast get-together the next week, Willie and I bantered ideas to initiate that specific action.

Willie suggested that we recruit Dana as an apprentice leader to work with Rose, me and all who were curious about internet dating sites. We both agreed that any support could be a tremendous help to a novice dater.

I remarked "Willie, you are so good with the newbie widows to give them encouragement to come through our door. I may be better at giving them the wings to exit." We both laughed. I continued, "This will give me an opportunity to share how valuable reconnecting with old friends can be. Others in the group may have old acquaintances that they would like to contact for a catch-up conversation. At the least, they might be open to talking if an old love or old friend should contact them."

I volunteered, "I will be willing to host an orientation meeting at my home on Valentine's Day to allow Rose a time to explain the value of internet dating. For those that are inspired to take the first step, other friends can volunteer to be a dating-partner. Follow-up sessions may be needed in my home on a regular basis to provide guidance and encouragement. Anything after the initial meeting will be a learning-as-we-go adventure."

I felt the inspiration was God's way of saying, "For those whose widowhood journey is best lived out by finding male companionship, this is a positive way to begin the search."

This idea had all the elements of an adventure with God

1. Inspiration from a divine source

2. Purpose to help others be all God created them to be

3. A level of excitement that is hard to contain

4. A method to help a fellow soul sister take steps through an adventuresome 'door' on her individualized journey

5. A need for God to be intricately involved to reach any successful result

Prayer to God:

WOW! God, your inspirations are always super-charged and mind-shocking. We will all need You for this mighty endeavor. Please, do not let us be afraid of magnificent success! I implore You to be very active in tending to our Butterfly Garden as we help others explore their own adventures. Especially stay close and involved should anyone choose to find a romantic love! That will definitely, become a "God help us" journey.

Dear Child,
Don't force these adventures. What will be, will be. Encourage your friends to be willing to step out in faith and trust that I will not lead them into a harmful situation. This requires that, like

you, they will need to depend on My guidance, and have the confidence that I am sending guidance during every choice that they make and action that they take.

Chapter 27

Tending A Butterfly Garden

2019

Eight ladies came to our "Learning to Date" talk. Unfortunately, Rose was ill, but Dana and I shared her wonderful experience finding someone at the age of 75. Some of the eight were merely curious, some were hopeful, and some wanted to watch the stories unfold. For those that were serious, we stayed after others had left and helped them set up their profile on a dating site. Once the profile was on its way to the dating site, we discussed what might happen next.

These are a few of the precautions we advised:

- Trust the rules of the site and don't give out phone numbers, address or personal information such as place of work. Women have had a rebuffed admirer show up at the home or office.
- Meet in a public place and drive self to the location. Pay for your own food or drink. Dana and I were available to sit in the corner and watch the interplay the first couple of meetings. I also read some of the early texts to determine the sincerity of the guy. I was fairly good at spotting a "player" -- someone who was dating more than one woman and in the game for entertainment, not commitment.
- Tell a friend exactly where you are going and who you will be with.

- Don't be afraid to fact check someone that you might have feelings for.
- Back out immediately if someone requests money for any reason.
- Anyone interested in dating should also consider the old way of meeting someone by introduction through a mutual friend.

The winks and clicks began for some of our widows. One of the women dated three different men. She found the conversations stimulating and learned that she still enjoyed conversing with a male. Unfortunately, all the guys used pictures from 10 years back when they were healthy and less heavy.

One found that it took her less time to learn the dating routine at this age than when she started dating in her teens. She became discerning and comfortable meeting new people. Although she didn't meet another she felt was a long-term companion, she moved out of the widowhood circle into the life of a single.

After a year, Willie and I had another breakfast discussion about the success of our dating adventure. We both agreed that some women need to try to date but won't persevere, some might if the right person showed up on their doorstep, and some will actively search as we all did before we settled on our husbands. We had several women move out of our group when they found a male companion. It was all good because others new to widowhood joined our circle of friends to find acceptance and respect…

When I was honest about my conversations with friends who happened to be male and my enjoyment catching up with those friends, other women felt sufficiently comfortable to admit that they also were conversing with old friends on a regular basis. We agreed that conversations with men could be comforting and enjoyable. The male-female dynamic is God's creation and doesn't need to fall away because a spouse has departed. The male viewpoint can be especially valuable when buying a car, selling a house, or describing a clunk-clunk noise under the hood of the car.

Chapter 28

A Little Story About 'Change'

2020
Ten Years A Widow

According to the dictionary, the word 'change' has more than one meaning:

verb

1.
make or become different.
Widowhood requires that women **change**.

2.
take or use another instead of.
She decided to **change** shoes.

noun

1.
the act or instance of making or becoming different.
the **change from** being married to being single

2.
coins as opposed to paper currency.
She found **change** in her car.

As I walked this morning on this beautiful day in early summer, I reflected on 'change'.

Initially in my life, the change from a married person to a widow was precisely the act of making or becoming different. In fact, most widows I have asked, feel like a completely different person after being widowed for a few years. That in itself is not good or bad, just different.

I take the same path 90% of the time. Today the changes in that walk were brought to my mind because I found a dime in the same driveway that I walked past yesterday. Overnight, this driveway changed from no dime to one dime. Today a coin, a piece of change appeared on the asphalt. And that dime went from a noun on the ground to a verb in my pocket as it worked to change my mind about 'changes'.

I reflected on everything I had witnessed since March of this year: the temperature, the awakening of the trees and grass, and the pattern of the sun. I had been able to note the seasonal patterns on a daily basis, from bleak branches in the winter to beautiful blossoms of many different colors signaling spring, to a vast display of leaves in all colors of green heralding the advent of summer. I remembered thinking that I was sad when the petals from the blossoms covered the pavement as they died away. And yet today, my path was alive with flowering bushes and stalks of lilies in several different colors. If the blossoms hadn't fallen away, the majestic tree foliage would not have arrived to provide the wonderful shade that I utilize to stay cool. For nature, change is good, but what about humans?

I recently have seen yard signs along my path: "Congrats' Class of 2020". Several Seniors are no longer students in High School. Although a little scary, that change of status will provide opportunities foundational to the rest of their lives. As I walked by those houses two weeks ago, I said a little prayer that each of those students would embrace this new opportunity and make good choices.

Other signs, along my two-mile walk in my neighborhood, indicated that several families were in the middle of a moving adventure. I saw the "For Sale" signs appear followed by sold banners a few days or weeks later. One can only hope that this obvious major event in the lives of these people would bring hope and prosperity. Certainly, each move would evoke some amount of added stress to their lives for a period of time.

This walk today put my mind in racing gear. And in the forefront was the reality of change for men and women who have lost a spouse. The saying by the Greek philosopher, Heraclitus was so very accurate, "Change is the only constant in life." It will take time and require purposeful decisions to eventually replace the grief with a plethora of wonderful memories. People do not need to carry their grief with them for the rest of their lives. If a friend or counselor states that, they are not being truthful.

Back to the dime that started this little mental meandering. It is a piece of change, a coin, that can make us and inspire us to become different. On each coin in America is stamped, "In God We Trust." That phrase is not there by accident. It is a reminder that we don't have to undergo any transformation by ourselves. The source of all change is God and He promises to carry us over the hurdles, and clear of the boulders if we will let him. On this, I speak from experience.

Chapter 29

A Godly Purpose Is The Best Adventure

2020
Ten Years A Widow

My purpose is to share my story with the hope that many widows will choose to recreate themselves. Widowhood truly is a new beginning. It is the chance for a widow to become whomever she desires to be. I realize that endeavor is not easy. My mother-in-law remained so despondent after her husband died, that her health deteriorated causing her own demise in 11 months. We tried everything we knew how to do, including moving her in with us to procuring an assisted-living apartment near her friends. Her broken heart could not be mended on this side of Heaven.

I would be so pleased if anyone who reads my story would be willing to take some simple steps to start his/her own personal adventure. Pondering thoughts and feelings can be beneficial. I have dumped everything into my journaling: questions, frustrations, choices, dreams, and decisions. Starting a journal of favorite memories can be notes in a book, scribblings on paper, a scrapbook, or actual files with notes on the computer.

I always smile when a desperate woman ventures into a new widow's support group. If the first group turns out to be peppered with women wearing a desperate widow demeanor, I hope the next group will be more optimistic. If a Braveheart wants to find adventuresome women, she may need to start her own group using some of the constructs that made our group so successful. I sense that it may be a situation that is built on faith. We started with four and have had consistently 15-25 people at our monthly luncheons for five years. The women who stayed with us were those who were ready to move on. I have enclosed questions for discussion at the end of this book. Doing a four-week book discussion with other widows may open discussions as my probing questions did for our group.

Many of my friends are finding their own purposes. Willie elected not to move out of town with her son and family because her friends were here. One widow has chosen to find homes for stray kittens. Those babies are her purpose. Several others are vitally involved with their grandchildren. One volunteered three days-a-week in our church office. Another opened her home to teach women how to quilt and knit. No one way fits all.

That leads into my closing thoughts. I hope my adventure with God is believable or I have failed. I have learned to see God working on my behalf, prodding me onward to new challenges. He will and does do that for every widow. He knows where the strengths and gifts lie for every person. If one will start down the path prompted by the stirrings in the heart, He will either correct a misstep or open the doors to expand the adventure. That is how I got to the Mountain Top and realized that Widowhood could be Wonderful. God's Biblical message is "seek and you will find, ask and the door will be opened unto you."

The type of relationship will be personal. I choose to meditate with God and listen purposefully as my form of communication. Others get their direction from the Bible or messages from their pastors. Still others find meaning and inspiration from great books by religious scholars. God is big. He will respond in a way that His listener will best be able to hear and comprehend. He only asks that to start, a seeker be willing to acknowledge that He is real. The rest of the journey will unfold.

My faithful God,

Thank You for leading me to a better understanding of Your desire to have personal relationships with all Your cherished children: God moments, adventures, as I have labeled them for years. You used my experiences of loss and overcoming to help others who may need to witness my journey.

Thank you for being my God. Thank you for taking me to the Mountain Top as You promised many years ago. My gift to You is my words of admiration and devotion. I offer my willingness to share our remarkable friendship with others. One day, I look forward to flying into Your arms with the fiercest hug I could possibly give to You.

Now that I accept that every moment of every day, You, God, have cherished me, I have the freedom to let go and let my world unfold as it should. To worry or speculate does not honor You. I am sorry it took me so long to recognize Your unfailing love for me. With that wisdom, I will try to give away all the love You have poured into me, onto others.

With all my heart,
Your Child

Dear Sweet Child,

I also enjoyed working this task with you, teasing the story out of the depths of your soul. I always knew it was there, even if you did not remember Who I am.

Yes, many are ignorant of My intentions and have forgotten that they also have a story with Me which began before they came into this life. I want all My children to realize who they are, and why they are who they are. That can only happen when they understand who I am.

I want My blessed children to come to Me excitedly, to be willing to have Mountain Top adventures all of their days on earth. That is

only possible through the power of unconditional love. Your recommendation for granting Me Free Will sums up My purposes quite nicely. Thank you for persevering in your efforts to define what it means for each person to love herself fully with a genuine belief that I will work tirelessly to help her be the best she can be.

Regardless of what happens with the book we have created; the story is now a part of you and will spill out onto others at just the time in their lives when they need to hear that a forever-love adventure with their cherished God is worth the challenge.

Your Best Friend,

Chapter 30

A Disclaimer

I am not a pastor and do not wish to undermine anyone's theology. I have been involved with a sufficient number of churches in my 70+ years to understand that many doctrines prevail. Some are validated by the Bible, others are not. Many churches espouse the need to ask for forgiveness for all our sins and to ask Christ to be our Savior. That is an excellent first step for many people.

These are my life stories. Communicating directly with my Abba Father gives me direction and peace of mind. My stories have attempted to explain how I learned to love a God who was constantly loving me first without judging all my missteps along the way. I have experienced consequences for bad choices, many that a good father would advise against continuing.

In this disclaimer, I am advocating that my God would never tell me to do anything that is unlawful or hurtful to another living person or creature. God would never advocate anything that violates His Ten Commandments as listed in Exodus 20:2-17, RSV of the Bible.

Judy Towne Jennings

About The Author

Judy Towne Jennings enjoyed a career as a physical therapist before life's challenges took her down the paths of caregiving and then widowhood. During those crises, her sense of self departed with the loss of her husband. Writing her first book, *Living with Lewy Body Dementia, One Caregiver's Personal, In-Depth Experience* helped her find a sense of purpose.

With this second book, she chronicles how she managed to create an improved version of her former self throughout her widowhood journey. Judy has had a passion to fix what is broken: her patients, her husband, and now the societal perspectives constraining widows and widowers. Too often, she felt that she was expected to wear the label of a poor, unfortunate widow for the rest of her life. That is not her nature.

She endorses a life of ambitious adventures orchestrated by the God of the Universe that may include passion and breath-taking moments. Her life has been filled with big and little amazing miracles. If this can happen to her, it can happen for anyone.

This book is Judy's loving message to all widows and lonely seniors everywhere. "We are meant to have full joyful lives for as long as we remain on this side of Heaven."

Potential Group Discussion Questions

1. Is Judy's loss of her identity a typical experience for other widows?

2. Is Judy's perception that other people were treating her differently a unique experience? Share similar or different personal experiences.

3. Does a form of noting, or journaling prove beneficial for anyone in the group? How does it differ from Judy's form of letter writing to her God living in her computer?

4. Two very different types of support groups were described in this story. How were they different and what type of widows might be drawn to each?

5. Several of the widows in Judy's group found they overcame their grief more easily by moving away from the city where they lived as a married couple. Discuss why.

6. Others did not stay in the group for various reasons. Discuss whether making big changes helps or hinders the struggle to overcome grief?

7. Judy claims to have God moments. Does God perform personal interactions in people's lives today, in your experience? Can miracles really happen for people?

8. Judy had a cathartic moment on the mountain. Share within the group any personal moments that changed the way you saw your

life unfolding. Does reading this story help you accept that the Holy Spirit might also be working in your life?

9. Discuss your reaction to a sick spouse or adult child rejecting the idea of dating for the one left behind?

10. Within your community, are widowed adults encouraged to seek another relationship or are they told that they are strong persons and do not need any other love partners in their lives?

11. Does anyone know a friend who had to "live in silver sin" because he or she would lose financial benefits if remarrying?

12. What does the author mean by saying that I learned to give God the gift of Free Will? What does Free Will mean within your faith?

13. Discuss your opinion of the comment **"What God didn't own was her willingness to let Him into her world."** Do you agree or disagree that a person can give God the gift of Free Will?

14. Judy talks about having an adventure with God? Discuss having that perspective in your group. What might change? Is Frank an adventure, in your opinion?

15. How would life change if we believed that God had our Backs, and there was no reason to worry?

Interesting reactions precipitated within a group discussion are welcome on Facebook.com/dementiacaregiver/ or Judytownejennings@gmail.com

Printed in the United States
By Bookmasters